DATE DUE

DEMCO

EXORCISM

FACT OR FICTION

EXORCISM

FACT OR FICTION

DR. KEN OLSON

THOMAS NELSON PUBLISHERS
NASHVILLE

The case histories described in this book are actual experiences of Dr. Olson's patients. Their names have been changed to protect their identities.

Published in Nashville, Tennessee, by Thomas Nelson, Inc., and distributed in Canada by Lawson Falle, Ltd., Cambridge, Ontario.

Scripture quotations are from the NEW KING JAMES VERSION of the Bible, copyright © 1979, 1980, 1982, Thomas Nelson, Inc., Publishers, and The Holy Bible: NEW INTERNATIONAL VERSION, copyright © 1978 by the New York International Bible Society, and are used by permission of Zondervan Bible Publishers.

Scripture quotations noted TLB are from *The Living Bible* (Wheaton, Illinois: Tyndale House Publishers, 1971) and are used by permission.

Library of Congress Cataloging-in-Publication Data

Olson, Ken.
    Exorcism : fact or fiction? / Ken Olson.
        p.   cm.
    Includes bibliographical references.
    ISBN 0-8407-3403-4 (pbk.)
    1. Exorcism—United States—Case studies.   2. Demoniac possession-
    -United States—Case studies.   I. Title.
    BV873.E8047   1992
    265'.94—dc20   92–18489
                                                                                CIP

Printed in the United States of America

1 2 3 4 5 6 7 — 97 96 95 94 93 92

To the God of Love
who heals the brokenhearted
and sets the captives free.

ACKNOWLEDGMENTS

I give special thanks to all who assisted me in writing this book: Marion Johnson, who has great skill in transferring my hand-written copy to the typed page; Ron Haynes, Al Ells, Janes Jones, and Patty Moore for their help in rewriting and editing this book.

I especially thank God for my wife, Jeannie. Little did we know what God had in store for us when we were married August 22, 1951, just before leaving for seminary in Minneapolis, Minnesota. After eleven years in the parish ministry, she supported my decision to go to graduate school to earn a doctorate in counseling psychology. We had three children by then and limited financial resources. When I was forty-five, I asked her how she felt about my closing my private practice for three years of independent study. She said, "I'm used to you starting over." The three years became seven years, as I spent the last four as an amateur detective trying to help get a friend freed from death row after he'd been convicted of a murder I believed he didn't commit. We received many threats to our lives at that time.

Then God called me back into the ministry of healing the brokenhearted and exorcism. Jeannie was confused and angry at me and God when I became an exorcist, and I couldn't blame her. But God in His loving grace has healed and blessed our marriage. We are more in love with each other now than ever before.

The words in 1 Peter 1:6–7 apply to us. "In this you greatly rejoice, though now for a little while you may have had to suffer grief in all kinds of trials. These have come so that your faith, of greater worth than gold, which perishes even though refined by fire, may be proved genuine and may result in praise, glory, and honor when Jesus Christ is revealed."

CONTENTS

FOREWORD

GOD IS FULL of wonderful surprises! I've often said that, and I believe it's true. Yet God gave me one surprise that I'm not so sure is wonderful. Had I planned my life of ministry and service myself, I wouldn't have expected Him to call me into exorcism—nor would I have chosen it.

My Pilgrimage

I have always been a people person, and perhaps that is partly what drew me to the ministry. Following my graduation from Northwestern Lutheran Theological Seminary in Minneapolis, where I received an excellent theological education, I served as a Lutheran pastor for eleven years in California. During those years I was drawn more and more to counseling. In order to develop my counseling skills, I enrolled in graduate courses in psychology and read numerous books on psychotherapy. Those experiences led me to pursue a doctorate in counseling at Arizona State University. I interned in the children's psychiatric unit of Arizona State Hospital in Phoenix and completed my doctoral degree in 1967.

I was employed as a psychologist at Arizona State Hospital and Camelback Psychiatric Hospital, and I founded the

Creative Living Foundation for the treatment of drug abusers. In private practice I counseled families and teenagers,
did marriage counseling, and worked with all the problems that psychotherapists usually see.

In 1975 I closed my clinical practice and I was able to
take time off for independent study. I was intensely interested in the healing of the whole person: emotionally, mentally, physically, nutritionally, and spiritually. Although my
theological background did not emphasize it, I had always
been curious about divine healing. I had been turned off by
the style and teaching of popular "faith healers," but had a
desire to know more about the inner healing of emotions
and memories, and to investigate the reality of physical
healing as well. I had no interest in exorcism!

Through my reading, I became acquainted with the
teachings of Agnes Sanford and Francis MacNutt, and was
very impressed with both. They appealed to my intellect,
yet seemed to be humble people who could laugh at themselves. Their ministries bore fruit, and their theology was
believable.

Somewhere during this part of my pilgrimage, I felt God
urging me to go back into the ministry. And I sensed His
prompting to be involved in a ministry of healing, although
I argued long and hard with God about this. It just didn't
fit my image of myself! In the summer of 1981, my pastor
asked me to consider becoming an assistant pastor to create
a Christian counseling center at the church. Since I had
viewed this as the goal of my doctorate, I was overjoyed.
"How do you feel about my praying for the sick?" I asked
my pastor. "Oh, that's all right with me," he said.

In the fall of that year I opened the Center for Living,
with a special ministry of healing the whole person, emotionally, mentally, spiritually, and physically, according to
the teachings and example of Jesus Christ. I received no
salary from the church but earned my income from fees for
counseling.

God's Big Surprise

As a young Roman Catholic priest, Francis MacNutt developed a healing and deliverance ministry that gained national attention. Eventually he left the priesthood and married, but his ministry continued to flourish. He is a gifted writer and teacher and travels all around the country giving workshops and seminars on healing.

I had always wanted to meet Francis, and I invited him and his wife, Judith, to Phoenix for a healing seminar. To my great joy, they agreed to come at the end of January 1982. During their visit I told Francis of my plan to start a Sunday night service offering prayer for the sick. I was quite surprised when he told me that we should be prepared for people who have demons to come to the services and need the healing of deliverance. I believed Francis, but I did not look forward to those experiences.

The Sunday night services began and the people began to come. Although the numbers remained small, they came from many different churches. Some even came great distances. And very soon the first person needing an exorcism appeared, and then another, and another. At first I believed that only occasionally would a person need an exorcism, but I was wrong. Of those who came, the percentage needing deliverance was very high. In fact, I began to complain to God, "Why me? I prayed for the gifts of healing, not for the work of an exorcist." Yet the Lord continued to send people to me, even from clear across the country, who were terribly wounded, emotionally, mentally, physically, and spiritually, and were in need of the healing of deliverance from evil spirits.

I began to read every book on inner healing and deliverance I could find, but I found less help than I hoped for and certainly less than I needed. Next I searched the Scriptures as never before, relying on the Holy Spirit to teach me. As I went through the process of inner healing and exorcism with those the Lord sent to me, I found more and more that I needed to rely on the anointing and power of the Holy Spirit.

My prayer life changed profoundly. Since I felt so powerless on my own, I began to learn how to be a prayer warrior in spiritual battle. I was in the midst of a spiritual war with demonic forces, and I was on a crash course of spiritual growth.

Fact or Fiction

The whole topic of evil, Satan, demons, and exorcism is a very uncomfortable subject for most people. The world of the supernatural evokes a wide range of reactions, from fear to fascination, belief to skepticism, curiosity to revulsion.

There has been a phenomenal rise in the occult, the New Age movement, satanism, and witchcraft. Rarely does a week go by without a newspaper or television report on some bizarre murder believed to have been committed by a satanist. In the past few years mental health professionals have also been hearing bizarre stories from adult survivors of satanic ritual abuse. These stories are so horrifying that therapists are in turmoil trying to determine if what they are hearing is fact or fantasy. A basic problem is that modern psychology leaves little room for the spiritual realm, and most therapists don't believe in evil spirits. One psychologist who works with ritual abusers was interviewed for an article in *The Arizona Republic*. The therapist, Dr. Holiday Milby, boldly stated, "I don't believe in all that demonic stuff. They're sociopaths."[1]

While these stories have been making news, the Christian church has been generally reluctant to see and deal with this spiritual war. For most of my professional life as a Lutheran pastor and a clinical psychologist I never bothered to think seriously about demonic possession and exorcism. Since I wasn't looking for the possibility of demon oppression and possession, I have since wondered how many people whom I saw in therapy were in need of deliverance while I was blind to their condition.

Declaring oneself to be an exorcist is bound to cause controversy, and I have had my share of it. Many have been skeptical or openly opposed to the work. I have chosen to go into independent ministry, free of denominational ties, in order to remain true to God's call in my life. It has been a lonely life for me from a human point of view. There is much I would like to share with others, but few would believe the experiences I have had. Yet I have discovered that Satan, the demonic realm, and the ministry of exorcism are *fact,* not fiction. There are realities that the church and individual Christians need to come to terms with.

I have been working on the cutting edge of a psychology of evil since 1982. But nothing in my psychological or theological training prepared me for this "far country." In fact, in many ways I had to unlearn a great deal in both areas before I could be effective. My purpose in making my experiences known now is simply to unmask the satanic realm and equip other Christians to battle against it. I want to see a powerful church actively engaged in healing the wounded and setting the captives free.

A Word of Caution

I have written this book because of my desire to mobilize the church in resisting Satan and healing his victims. Readers should know, however, that the case histories and examples in this book are extremely graphic. Many people, on first being exposed to the facts of satanism, are shocked and frightened. I do not relish having to repeat some of the horrible things that satanists have done, but I firmly believe that if we fear to publicly expose it, the evil will continue and grow. Sometimes it is difficult to get the horror of it all out of your mind. As a professional who deals daily with the demonic world, I have learned to distance myself from it in order to keep my emotional sanity. As a reader being exposed to it for the first time, you may not be able to do this. If you find you have difficulty coping with these facts, ask someone to pray with you. Arm yourself with prayer and the truth of God's Word and the ultimate victory of Christ. If need be, put the book down for a time or skip to the chapters on healing for the information you need.

I have grown to appreciate Martin Luther and his great hymn of spiritual warfare, "A Mighty Fortress Is Our God." The third stanza has been especially meaningful to me:

> And tho' this world with devils filled,
> Should threaten to undo us,
> We will not fear, for God hath willed
> His truth to triumph through us.
> The Prince of Darkness grim—
> We tremble not for him;
> His rage we can endure,
> For lo, his doom is sure,
> One little word shall fell him.[2]

PART ONE

SPIRITUAL WARFARE

For we do not wrestle against flesh and
blood, but against principalities, against
powers, against the rulers of the darkness
of this age, against spiritual hosts of
wickedness in the heavenly places.

(Eph. 6:12)

1

MY NAME IS LEGION

I HAD AN ominous feeling inside when I heard the phone ringing at 7:00 A.M. A woman introduced herself as Sue, saying, "I'm calling for a friend who is terrified and desperate. He believes he is possessed by demons, and he urgently needs help."

With a sinking feeling in the pit of my stomach, I asked her, "How can I help?"

"Do you know Francis MacNutt's phone number in Florida? I want to call and ask him to perform an exorcism on my friend Mark."

Sue reported she had attended the healing seminar that Francis gave in Phoenix in 1982. I breathed a sigh of relief and gladly said, "Yes, I have his phone number. Hold on, and I'll get it for you."

About half an hour later, my phone rang again. Again it was Sue.

"Ken, Francis won't be able to perform the exorcism. I asked him who he would recommend in the Phoenix area, and he recommended you."

Mark's Story

At 6:30 that evening Sue and Mark arrived at my office. I had invited John, a friend of mine, to assist in the exorcism.

Mark was a handsome man in his mid-thirties, 6'3" tall, weighing about 225 pounds. Feeling a bit intimidated by his size, I prayed silently that this would not be a violent exorcism.

Mark gave a deep sigh of exhaustion as he sank into a chair. There were dark circles under his bloodshot eyes. The muscles in his forehead and jaws were tense from too much stress. When he spoke, his voice revealed fear and anxiety. The words tumbled out in an uninterrupted flow, releasing some long-building tension as he told his story.

"I don't know where to begin. I've been under so much pressure and stress the past few years. I went through a very difficult and painful divorce, my construction company went broke, and my father died after ten years of being an invalid. I'm exhausted by working from 4:30 in the morning until I drop at night. And I have a serious problem with alcohol.

"Emotionally I'm a time bomb ready to explode with hate, resentment, rage, guilt, fear, anxiety, and hopelessness. How is that for emotional problems? Fear and anxiety have taken me over totally.

"Worst of all, I have a real problem with sex. I'm obsessed with compulsive sexual thoughts and lust for women. Yet intercourse brings me only a little relief. I can't get enough sex or be satisfied with any woman, and I feel a lot of anger toward all women.

"Ten years ago I got married. It was a real disaster. She drank a lot. I can remember her being drunk at nine in the morning. After a few drinks she would go into a violent rage as if she were bent on destroying me—and she almost did during the divorce and custody hearing. I gave her everything. I agreed to pay child support that was more than I was earning. We were divorced three years ago after seven hellish years of marriage."

Mark went on to describe his increasing addiction to alcohol as he struggled with his father's lengthy and expensive illness and the failure of his construction business. In desperation, he finally cried out to Jesus and had a powerful "mountaintop" experience of spiritual elation. Yet his drinking continued, and as he tried to stabilize his spiritual life by attending church, he experienced tremendous spiritual opposition.

"I would stand at the front door of the church and something would come over me, trying to keep me from entering. It seemed so strange. I couldn't figure out what was wrong."

When Mark was able to go to church, he felt like he was on a roller coaster of emotional ups and downs. In response to powerful preaching, he often cried convulsively and would experience some peace, but the turmoil and anxiety quickly returned.

"One Sunday in November 1981 I came to the decision that I wanted to go to the altar and publicly accept Jesus Christ as my personal Savior, but I couldn't leave the pew. Some force was holding me back. It wasn't until February 1982 that I could finally walk forward during an altar call and accept Jesus as my Lord and Savior. A month later I was baptized."

After his baptism Mark experienced about a month of peace and serenity, and life seemed worth living again. He came out of his shell and began dating a Christian woman, until their relationship hit a snag.

"I wanted to have sex with her, but she refused to sleep with me before marriage. I became angry with God, and said 'If I have to give up sex, then I don't want You.'" Mark started to backslide rapidly and began drinking again. Compulsively he sought sexual partners and then felt sick about it. His mind was confused, and he could barely function at work. When he tried to read his Bible, there seemed to be a powerful force inside him that didn't want him to read; his thinking would become so muddled that the words made no sense.

Finally, one night Mark had the first of a series of bizarre experiences. While driving home, something strange began to happen. "There was the sound of a hard wind blowing, but there was no wind. As I approached my house, there was an eeriness about it, and suddenly I was filled with fear. Something was wrong. A voice told me to go into the house. I had a premonition of death, and a chill went up and down my body. When I got inside I sensed a heavy presence in the living room, a suffocating presence. My home was icy cold, especially the living room. Something was there!"

Suffering from near exhaustion, Mark tried to go to sleep, but felt the icy presence move into his bedroom. Filled with terror, he thought perhaps some medicine would help him sleep. Heading for the medicine cabinet, he caught a glimpse of himself in the mirror.

"My eyes were glazed over, and my face began to change into that of a very old man, covered with wrinkles, who looked a hundred years old. He was tired and weary looking, yet there was a wild look in his eyes. I wasn't drunk; in fact I'd had nothing to drink that day."

Returning to his bedroom, Mark sensed a presence on the edge of his bed. Numb with fear, he said "I belong to Jesus Christ. You can't have me!" The presence left the bedroom and a peace came over Mark, but this was not the end of his story.

He awoke the next morning to a beautiful day and began to reflect on the previous night's events. Suddenly the intense cold returned, and he felt all his energy and strength drain away.

"I grabbed my Bible and lay back on the bed. I had never been so fatigued or weak in my life. All at once there was a huge, heavy presence sitting on my rib cage, crushing the air out of me. I passed out and went into a deep sleep."

The days and weeks that followed were filled with incredible turmoil. Emotionally Mark felt like a powerful volcano ready to erupt. Fear and anxiety overwhelmed him. He had quit drinking, but he began again more heavily than ever. His powerful lust for women returned with a murderous rage.

"One day while drinking, I was holding a .357 Magnum and felt an overwhelming desire to kill my former wife. I finally lay down on my bed, and a deep voice rose up out of me. 'I am Legion. I am Legion!' it said.

"The words came out of my mouth, but the voice was not mine. I shook all over and tried to say 'Jesus,' but I couldn't. Then there spewed forth from me horrible and blasphemous words against God. I couldn't stop the words coming out of my mouth. I was finally able to say 'Jesus,' and the voice stopped."

Mark plunged into more drinking and greater confusion. He was afraid to go to church because of the horrible language that might come out of his mouth. With visible distress, he neared the end of his story.

"This morning I woke up to the heavy presence of evil in my house. From deep inside of me came this strange voice again, saying, 'I am Legion!'" He looked at me with pleading eyes. "I can't handle this any longer. I don't think I'm crazy. I believe a spiritual battle is being waged over me. I called Sue and begged her to find someone to help me before it's too late."

Fighting for Mark

The sun was setting as we entered the church sanctuary. The last rays of sunlight illuminated the stained-glass windows with their brilliant colors. I asked Sue, Mark, and John to sit in the front pew while I prayed over the church building, commanding in the name of Jesus Christ that all demonic spirits in the sky above and the ground beneath the building be bound from hindering us. I also rebuked all demonic spirits in the church building and commanded them to leave and go back to the bottomless pit. Then I prayed to God, asking Him to protect the church with the blood of Jesus Christ.

I said prayers over us and the neighborhood, claiming the protection of the blood of Christ and asking for the power of the Holy Spirit to cover us, surround the church, and fill us. Then I prayed against all the demonic spirits possessing Mark.

Mark's head had remained bowed, and when I finished praying he lifted it. His eyes were fixed on me. They began to change, becoming filled with evil and hate, and his features took on the look of a dark, sinister presence. It was an awesome thing to witness.

Then, from the very depths of his being, came a thunderous, rolling voice crying out and reverberating from the church walls, "Oh, my God. Oh, my God!" I'd never heard such a loud and powerful voice before. I could see a demon staring at me through Mark's eyes. A forceful growl declared, "I am Legion," and the powerful spiritual battle of exorcism began.

I had no fear, nor have I ever been afraid during an exorcism. The presence and power of the Holy Spirit give me a source of strength and peace.

The hours went by very quickly. During a quiet time when Mark was lying on the floor resting, a demon spoke through him, saying, "Are they all gone?"

"No," I said, "and you can go now." (There's nothing like a little comic relief in the midst of a grim battle.)

When most of the legion of demons seemed to have left him, Mark stood before a large wooden cross hanging on the wall, his hands reaching out to it. Suddenly, a very powerful demon gripped him, twisting his body. As I faced this stubborn entity, I prayed to the Father to send us Michael. Sensing the aid of the heavenly powers, I commanded the demon to leave, and, with a final scream that caused Mark to double over with pain, it departed.

In the aftermath we laid Mark on the front pew and

placed our hands on him, praying for inner healing and the infilling of the Holy Spirit's power. Mark lay in exhaustion after his four-hour ordeal. Finally, he opened his eyes and thanked me.

"You are a powerful man of God," He said. "Satan hates you. You will go through some very difficult times and testing by Satan, but God will triumph in your life."

The next day we met at my office. Mark said he felt completely drained emotionally. He began to reflect on the night before.

"I vaguely remember walking out of the sanctuary. What happened to me? Was it because I was burned out from too much stress, or was it the side effect of too much alcohol? Was I psychotic and hallucinating all these experiences, or was it really an unbelievable, spiritual experience with the supernatural?"

IS IT REAL?

An encounter with the demonic during an exorcism has a surrealistic quality. On one hand, it exposes the evil that resides in the subconscious mind through sin and our fallen nature. At the same time, it confronts real, personal evil entities from the pit of hell.

I know that what I experience during a powerful exorcism is completely real. Yet afterward it seems so much like a dream, I feel it couldn't possibly have happened. Those who find deliverance through exorcism, with all its bizarre experiences, can also begin to doubt that it was real. Most Christians find it easier just to be "religious." We want to deal with the world of religious rituals and externals that are limited to our five senses, rather than with unseen realms. Yet the freedom, release, and joy that result from a powerful deliverance of the Holy Spirit testify to the reality of the experience. Lives that are healed and changed cannot be denied.

The resurgence of the demonic in our day will not fade away and must not be ignored. The occult, witchcraft, satanism, and other cultic practices are forcing the Body of Christ to respond, however reluctantly. Even the Roman Catholic Church has had to clarify its belief in the reality of the demonic, as Pope Paul VI explained in his address, "Deliver Us from Evil," in November 1972.

> What are the greatest needs of the church today? Do not let our answer surprise you as being oversimple or even superstitious and unreal! One of the greatest needs is defense from that evil which is called the devil. Evil is not merely a lack of something, but an effective agent, a living, spiritual being, perverted and perverting. . . .
>
> It is a departure from . . . biblical and church teaching to refuse to acknowledge the devil's existence or to explain the devil as a pseudo-reality, a conceptual, fanciful personification of the unknown causes of misfortunes. We are dealing not with just one devil, but with many. . . .
>
> Our doctrine becomes uncertain, obscured as it is by the darkness surrounding the devil. But our curiosity, excited by the certainty of his multiple existence, justifies two questions: Are there signs, and what are they, of the presence of diabolical action? And what are the means of defense against such an insidious danger?[1]

I am writing this book because I have faced the realities of the world of Satan and his demonic servants. I want to share with the world what I have learned and experienced in healing the brokenhearted and setting captives free from evil spirits. I am not writing from any denominational or doctrinal point of view, except I want to say that I have sought to be as grounded in the Holy Bible as I possibly can be.

As you read the remainder of this book, don't get the idea that exorcisms are all I do. Every day as a clinical psychologist I see people with normal problems who are in need of psychotherapy. This is how I earn my living. I am really a very normal man who has a wonderful wife, three great children who are now married, and seven delightful grandchildren. I love the Los Angeles Dodgers, the Phoenix Suns, pepperoni pizza, and lutefisk.

And my old saying, "God is full of wonderful surprises," is still true. Perhaps I wouldn't have chosen to be what some call a "ghostbuster." But I thank God continually for the privilege of sharing in His powerful work of exorcising evil through deliverance, healing, and the restoration of broken lives.

2

WORLDVIEWS AT WAR

He who comes to God must believe that
He is, and that He is a rewarder of those
who diligently seek Him.

(Heb. 11:6)

IN MY EARLY days in the pastorate, like most clergy, I
didn't pay much attention to Scripture passages that per-
tained to Satan and casting out demons. I ignored the topic
so well that for most of my years as a pastor I never
preached on the subject. Personally I was unsure about the
reality of Satan, evil spirits, and exorcism. I also had a pastoral concern that preaching on the subject could fill my
congregation with fear.

Fear is a common reaction to demonstrations of the awesome power of God. Even in New Testament times, the exorcism of demons caused fear in people's hearts. In the
gospel of Luke we find the story of Jesus' exorcism of a
man possessed of many demons called "Legion." We are
told that when the townspeople came to Jesus, "they found
the man from whom the demons had departed, sitting at
the feet of Jesus, clothed and in his right mind. And they

were afraid" (Luke 8:35). They immediately begged Jesus to leave the area, "because they were overcome with fear" (v. 37).

The 1973 release of the film *The Exorcist* thrust the whole topic of demon possession onto the center stage of American consciousness. Most of those who saw the film reacted with fear. It is the story of two priests seeking to deliver a young girl from the possession of demons and was actually based on a real-life story. The special effects portraying the bizarre changes in the girl's body were electrifying and a fairly realistic description of Satan's power. Unfortunately in the film version both priests are killed, and Satan has a victory. The actual events took place in the life of a teenage boy. He had opened himself to the manifestations of demonic spirits by playing with a Ouija board. The exorcism team worked intensively with the boy for four months before the battle was finished. God sent Michael to set the boy free and, contrary to the film story, the victory was Christ's, not Satan's.

We fear what we do not understand, and the fear of the satanic is part of our general uneasiness with the supernatural realm. I must admit that I was guilty of unbelief concerning the supernatural activity of God and Satan in daily life. As much as I value my theological education, the question of a personal devil, evil spirits, exorcisms, and healing was essentially ignored by my seminary professors. We did have lively discussions on the problem of evil, but they were more from a philosophical than a biblical point of view, and we were careful to keep them in the abstract. We concluded that "demon possession" and "exorcism" were concepts used in Jesus' time for describing how Jesus healed the mentally ill.

I was taught that the age of signs and wonders, such as healing miracles, had past. I believed God sent the Holy Spirit to start the Christian church, and His power was manifested in signs and wonders so that the world would know it was not merely the work of man. Once the Bible was completed and the church founded, however, the manifest power of the Holy Spirit was no longer needed, or so I assumed.

When I accepted these ideas into my belief system, it followed naturally that I did not pray for the sick to be miraculously healed, nor did I expect any supernatural encounters as part of my daily life.

REALITY IN A BUBBLE

I've come to realize that each Christian denomination develops its own "theological bubble." This is a view of the world that defines its reality, and within that view there are certain biblical truths that are emphasized more than others. We tend to notice and incorporate into our bubbles the things that support it, and we ignore the facts that don't. This is called "selective perception."

Western Scientific Thought

In order to understand how our bubbles, or worldviews, were developed, we have to go back in history. Christianity was born in an Eastern culture that was very comfortable with the ideas of both a visible and an invisible world. In Bible times, people could easily believe that unseen forces (such as angels, devils, or God) produced visible results. Disease or disaster were associated with sin or the attacks of the devil. This understanding of the world persisted through the early years of the church and into the Middle Ages. It was not until the sixteenth and seventeenth centuries and the rise of scientific theory and method that people's understanding of the world began to change. As some diseases and illnesses were traced to natural causes, such as germs, many scientists came to the conclusion that *all* visible phenomena had natural or explainable causes. As early as the mid-1500s, René Descartes and other philosophers proposed new worldviews that described the universe as a mechanical system in purely mathematical terms. They viewed the universe as a closed system in which reality consisted only of what could be seen, measured, or in some way proven empirically. As the discoveries of science made rapid progress, man, materialism, and scientism were exalted. By the time Charles Darwin came on the scene in the mid-1800s, the stage was set for an explanation of creation that completely left God out of the picture.

Modern Psychology

The field of psychology responded to this closed universe "bubble" by producing its own set of natural explanations for human behavior. Not just demons and the supernatural, but the very spiritual dimension of humankind is dismissed by many modern psychological theories. (I find it ironic that the very word psychology means, literally, "the study of the soul.")

Sigmund Freud, often considered the father of modern psychology, suggested that both God and Satan were mental substitutes for a human father. He concluded that what people once called evil spirits were really "base and evil wishes deriving from impulses which have been rejected and repressed."[1] What people in previous centuries had called demonic possession, Freud called neurosis. In short, he taught that possession by demons was the expression of the unruly id breaking through the control of the superego.

Carl Jung postulated the "collective unconscious," which is a storehouse of racial memories and impressions inherited by each person. He taught that the images in the collective unconscious are shaped by predispositions, called "archetypes." One of the archetypes proposed by Jung is the "shadow side," a facet of human personality that creates symbols of demons, devils, and evil ones. According to Jung, humans use these symbols to explain all of their own repressed and unacceptable motives, tendencies, and desires.[2]

The 1930s saw the rise of another popular psychological theory called "behaviorism." B. F. Skinner, its most prominent researcher and spokesman, sought to explain both animal and human behavior entirely in terms of the observable and measurable responses to stimuli. Skinner rejected the unobservable completely and based his work on the theory that what you can't see does not exist.

The 1900s also gave birth to the Humanist school of psychology, known for its person-centered approach, which elevates humans to the highest place in creation. In essence, humanistic psychologists see a core in each person that contains a powerful drive to realize his or her full potential and thus achieve self-actualization. This school of thought emphasizes the premise that everyone's feelings are legitimate and should be accepted unconditionally, leaving no room for absolute standards or yardsticks (for example, the Bible) by which we can measure ourselves. Demonic possession is viewed as a lack of growth, the inability to achieve self-esteem. In this view, society is the real demon we face, as it blocks the free expression of growth and creativity by the individual.[3]

In studying these psychological frameworks, it becomes clear that they leave no room in their bubbles for the invisible world of the supernatural. They relegate God, Satan, angels, and demons to the realm of fiction, not fact.

Changing Theology

The elevation of humans, materialism, science, and the philosophy of a closed universe began to have a powerful influence on the Church. Many theologians wanted respectability in an age of science, and they began to edge away from biblical truths. The use of reason to explain away miracles and reduce scriptural truths to the level of myths became common practice. One liberal theologian,

Rudolf Bultmann, became famous for "demythologizing" the Bible. In one of his books he said:

> The forces and the laws of nature we have discovered [show] we can no longer believe in spirits, whether good or evil. Sickness and the cure of diseases are likewise attributed to natural causation. They are not the result of demonic activity or evil spirits. The idea of Satan and demons is finished. Finished is the theory of the Virgin birth. Finished is the question of whether Jesus of Nazareth is God's son or not. Finished is the teaching of substitutionary atonement, the resurrection, and the ascension. Finished is the belief in the Second Coming. Finished are the miracles and answers to prayer. What is left of the Bible and the Christian faith is nothing but a myth. It is impossible to use electric light and the wireless and avail ourselves of modern medicine and surgical discoveries and at the same time to believe in the New Testament world of spirits and miracles.[4]

Today's Divergent Views

Although scientism and naturalism dramatically affected Western thought and life, they did not take over completely. The rise of the occult and the revival of Eastern mysticism indicate that people are still hungry for the supernatural and believe there is an invisible side to the universe. Even among the clergy, there are widely differing views on the subject.

The Arizona Republic featured an article by then religion editor Richard Lessner, entitled "Raising the Devil," which appeared in the May 21, 1983, issue. Lessner interviewed priests and pastors in the Phoenix area and explored the wide disagreement among the clergy on the role of demonology in their ministries. "Demons are not just something you traffic in every day," said the Rev. John Mitchell of Phoenix Bethany Bible Church. "I believe in the present reality of demons according to the Bible, but I think that they are more prevalent in societies where there is no high esteem for God like in our highly Christianized society."

"While I would not absolutely rule out the possibility of the existence of demons, demonology, possession and exorcisms, they do not play a significant role in my ministry," said the Rev. Steven Richardson of First Phoenix Christian Church.

"I do not have a theology which includes anything like that," was the comment of William Smith of Shadow Rock Congregational Church in North Phoenix. "There is no place in my theology for the demonic, for spiritual intervention in our lives. It's just contradictory to my world view."

On the other side Lessner found some pastors and Roman Catholic priests who not only believe in the reality of demons, but who practice deliverance of people from demonic spirits. Catholic Father McKinnon was quoted as saying, "There are two tremendous mistakes about Satan—to say he doesn't exist or attribute everything back to him. Jesus told us to watch out for three things: the world, the flesh, and the devil."

Dr. Hans Sebold, professor of sociology at Arizona State University and an authority on witchcraft and the occult told Lessner:

Modern beliefs in demons and demonic possession, as objective realities, and not just as a way of describing psychological ills, are explainable by the theory of "functional analysis." According to this interpretation, beliefs are explained by their actual function in society. . . .

No society has ever been wholly free of belief in demons. The mind and body will respond to the belief in demons as if they are real, so long as a person believes they are real. Profound belief creates its own reality. . . .

Within a scientific framework, there has not been a single verified, authenticated, scientifically described case of demon possession. All the manifestations attributed to demons are explainable in purely naturalistic terms. . . .

At the core of belief in demons is a predisposition to believe. This leads to selective perceptions, selective memory, selective distortion, and selective inattention to data. You simply select the information that confirms what you want to believe. Most people want confirmation of what they believe, so they ignore what contradicts that belief.[5]

Hans Sebold states the problem very well. Ironically, what he says about selective perception, confirming what you believe and ignoring whatever contradicts that belief, applies to most of modern science today. When science restricts reality only to that which is observable and measurable, it seriously reduces the size of the bubble in which it can operate. Of course science will find naturalistic explanations for demonic manifestations if it assumes beforehand that nothing can exist outside the physical world! When the spiritual is not included in your bubble, then no spiritual explanations will ever be advanced or accepted. They are, by definition, impossible.

MY TRANSFORMATION

I must admit that my theological education and the biblical scholarship I was taught affected my thinking and limited my theological bubble. Although I believed in the Holy Spirit, I didn't expect to see His power actively demonstrated in my daily life. I couldn't accept Bultmann's demythologizing the Bible, but I did tend to reduce Scripture to its smallest parts. I believed Satan existed and people could be filled with demons, but since I had never encountered Satan or demons, they did not play a major role in my worldview and belief system.

Although I was not ready to consign the demonic world to fiction, I had a hard time coming to grips with it as fact, since it had never been a fact of my own experience.

In a very real way, however, seeing is believing. When God brought me face to face with demonic entities, I was forced to change my old belief system to encompass this new reality. I went scurrying back to my Bible and to my knees to discover the truths that I had been "editing out" of Scripture. When you go through the experience of an exorcism, it changes not only your belief systems, but it changes you!

I began to appreciate in a new way the spiritual warfare of Martin Luther. He had many personal encounters with Satan, whose existence was as certain to him as his own. More than once Luther threw the inkstand at Satan. Luther's own doubts, carnal temptations, evil thoughts, and external enemies convinced him that he was a marked man, singled out by Satan for destruction.

Luther reported that Satan assumed visible form and appeared to him as a dog, a hog, a goat, or as a flame or star, and sometimes as a man with horns. Luther said, "He is noisy and boisterous and he is at the bottom of all witchcraft and ghost trickery."[6]

Luther also believed the devil has no real power over believers. Satan, he said, hates prayer, sacred music, the Cross, and the Word of God, which he flees as from a flaming fire. And if the Scripture will not expel him, jeering and taunting will. "The devil," Luther said, "will bear anything better than to be despised and laughed at."[7]

As I continued to learn and grow in this new realm of counseling and deliverance, I was relieved to find that I was not the only therapist who believed in the reality of possession. Dr. R. D. Laing is one maverick in psychotherapy. In his book *The Divided Self,* he wonders about "a most curious phenomenon of the personality, one which has been observed for centuries, but has not yet received its full explanation. [It] is that in which the individual seems to be the vehicle of a personality that is not his own.

Someone else's personality seems to 'possess' him, finding expression through his words and actions, whereas the individual's own personality is temporarily 'lost' or gone! This happens with all degrees of malignancy."[8]

Those in the mental health field, who have had to treat adults and children abused by satanic groups, have had no psychology of evil to guide them. The frightful reality of evil and demonic power manifested in today's world, however, is forcing men like Laing and many other psychological and ministerial professionals to change their views. The broken, devastated victims of Satan's cruelty compel us to seek a deeper understanding of evil and a more powerful means of treating its casualties. I can no longer afford to keep my safe bubble of a fictional devil with a cute red outfit, horns, and a tail. I have seen firsthand the tormented captives of the devil, and God has thrust me into confrontation with Satan, waging a life-or-death battle against his kingdom.

Psychologist Viktor Frankl perfectly describes where I am, and where others are, in an area he calls "medical ministry." He recognizes there is a dividing line between medicine and religion and that the scientific methods of medicine do not always apply to religion, just as some of the most basic tenets of religion do not translate into provable scientific fact based on the mass of knowledge we have today. The psychology of evil falls into the great divide that separates the two. It is an area we don't understand but must investigate and learn to deal with, for Satan and his evil forces are ever present. Frankl says, "Anyone who walks along the frontier between two countries must remember that he is under surveillance from two sides. Medical ministry, therefore, expects wary glances; it must take them into the bargain. Medical ministry lies between realms. It, therefore, is a border area and, as such, a no-man's-land."[9]

That the supernatural is fact is not in dispute. Our most compelling task now is to recognize evil for what it is and invade this no-man's-land, claiming it and all Satan's victims there, restoring them to Christ's kingdom.

3

WHO IS THE DEVIL?

He is a liar and the father of it.

(John 8:44)

AS GOD SENT me dramatic experiences of direct confrontation with demons, they popped my theological bubble and I was forced to go back to the Bible. I searched the Old and New Testaments, seeking to understand my adversary, the devil. Never before had I understood so clearly the nature of the spiritual warfare between God and Satan, and the way that warfare permeates the entire biblical record. From Genesis to Revelation, the presence of Satan is a potent force, seeking to destroy the people of God and the beauty of God's creation.

THE OLD TESTAMENT

Although mentioned in the Old Testament only a few times by the specific name of "Satan" (see 1 Chron. 21:1; Zech. 3:2; and Job 1:6), the devil is referred to continually by other names. He is called Lucifer, the Morning Star, the Son of the Dawn, and Beelzebub, the Lord of the Flies. He is portrayed throughout Scripture as a tempter, a deceiver, a liar, and a murderer, but he didn't start out that way.

The Beautiful Angel

Although we are not told explicitly the origin of Satan and his demons, the Scriptures give us some strong clues. Two passages in the Old Testament have long intrigued Bible scholars, and many believe they refer to Satan. Just as in the Psalms David often spoke of himself and at the same time prophetically of Christ, so also Ezekiel and Isaiah, delivering warnings to evil kings, seem under the prompting of the Holy Spirit to refer to the fall of Satan.

> You were the seal of perfection,
> Full of wisdom and perfect in beauty.
> You were in Eden, the garden of God;
> Every precious stone was your covering. . . .
> You were the anointed cherub who covers;
> I established you;
> You were on the holy mountain of God;
> You walked back and forth in the midst of fiery stones.
> You were perfect in your ways from the day you were
>   created,
> Till iniquity was found in you.
> By the abundance of your trading
> You became filled with violence within,
> And you sinned;
> Therefore I cast you as a profane thing
> Out of the mountain of God;
> And I destroyed you, O covering cherub,
> From the midst of the fiery stones.
> Your heart was lifted up because of your beauty;
> You corrupted your wisdom for the sake of your
>   splendor;
> I cast you to the ground.
>
> (Ezek. 28:12–17)

Isaiah echoes this tragic rebellion and fall of the once beautiful cherub:

> How you are fallen from heaven,
> O morning star, son of the dawn!
> You have been cast down to the earth,
> You who once laid low the nations!
> You said in your heart,
> "I will ascend to heaven;
> I will raise my throne
>   above the stars of God;
> I will sit enthroned on the mount of assembly,
>   on the utmost heights of the sacred
>   mountain.
> I will ascend above the tops of the clouds;
> I will make myself like the Most High."
> But you are brought down to the grave,
>   to the depths of the pit.
>
> (Isa. 14:12–15)

Satan was created a very beautiful angel and given a high rank of power in heaven. As a cherub he was near to the throne of God. Although he was blameless in the beginning, he did have a free will, and his fall came as a result of his lust for power and pride and his attempt to dethrone God. In Revelation we get a glimpse of the battle in heaven that came as a result of Satan's rebellion:

And war broke out in heaven: Michael and his angels fought against the dragon; and the dragon and his angels fought, but they did not prevail, nor was a place found for them in heaven any longer. So the great dragon was cast out, that serpent of old, called the Devil and Satan, who deceives the whole world; he was cast to the earth, and his angels were cast out with him.

(Rev. 12:7–9)

Scripture says that Satan and his rebellious angels were thrown out of heaven and have come to earth to lead the whole world astray. Verse twelve of the same chapter says, "Woe to the inhabitants of the earth and the sea! For the devil has come down to you, having great wrath, because he knows that he has a short time." Satan is jealous of God's love for man, and in his fury seeks to destroy humankind.

The Tempter of Man

The third chapter of Genesis tells of man's fall into sin. Satan didn't make the assault of his power and terror on Adam and Eve obvious because that would only have driven them to seek God's protection. Instead, his tempting Eve was seemingly harmless. "Now the serpent was more crafty than any of the wild animals the LORD God had made. He said to the woman, 'Did God really say, "You must not eat from any tree in the garden"?'" (v. 1).

Eve responded as though it were a silly question. "We may eat fruit from the trees in the garden," she said, and then she remembered, "but God did say, 'You must not eat fruit from the tree that is in the middle of the garden, and you must not touch it, or you will die'" (vv. 2–3).

First Satan feigned ignorance, and then he used doubt to suggest to Eve, "You will not surely die . . . for God knows that when you eat of it your eyes will be opened, and you will be like God, knowing good and evil" (vv. 4–5).

Wanting to be like God is the desire for ultimate power and self-exaltation. To be like God—to write my own laws, to be a law unto myself—is wanting to be able to do it my way. That was the rebellious choice Satan made in heaven and it led to his fall. It was man's choice and it led to his fall and a broken relationship with God. This choice is called *sin*.

We all know that Adam and Eve succumbed to Satan's temptation and ate the forbidden fruit. As a result, they were ejected from the garden of perfection into a life of struggle and pain. "And the LORD God said, 'The man has now become like one of us, knowing good and evil'" (v. 22). And, tragically, we have learned of good and evil. Rebellion, pride, and self-exaltation are the ongoing story of man. God created angels and humans with the free will to choose to worship and obey Him or to choose to rebel and play god ourselves.

Satan is at war with the children of God, and he is working overtime to tempt, to deceive, to lie to, to seduce, to accuse, to blind, to confuse God's people. Satan wants us to be laws unto ourselves, to rebel against God's Word and will, to glorify self, to satisfy our sensuous natures through lust, sex, pornography, and drugs. Ultimately, he wants us to worship him through the idolatry of the occult and to be *destroyed*. Satan doesn't worry about the person he already controls. Instead he attacks the one who answers God's call, seeking Him with his whole heart, mind, and spirit. Satan will do anything to prevent men and women from loving and obeying God.

At War with Israel

God spoke to Abraham and said, "I will make you a great nation; I will bless you . . . in you all the families of the earth shall be blessed" (Gen. 12:2-3).

The people of Israel were God's chosen people. Through them would come the Messiah, who would destroy the power of Satan. As you read the Old Testament, remember that a spiritual war is going on between the kingdom of God and the kingdom of darkness, between God's people and His adversary, Satan.

As in any war, there are casualties. The history of the people of Israel is filled with the casualties of this ongoing war. I used to wonder why God was so angry when the Israelites sinned by building idols of wood or gold. Isn't an idol just the result of man's imagination with no real power behind it? Now I realize that idolatrous worship is inseparable from demonic power. It is through this supernatural power that the Prince of Darkness can bring people into demonic bondage. The Bible plainly recognizes the spiritual entities behind the idols of heathenism and states that the power behind these entities is demonic.

We see a clear example of this demonic power in the history and biblical record of the Israelites' sojourn in Egypt.

The Israelites in Egypt

Egypt was a land of demonic powers and sorcerers who used black magick and the secret arts of the occult. (I use the spelling *magick,* with a *k,* to differentiate it from the sleight-of-hand type of magic used in show business today.) The Egyptian sorcerers, through their black magick, became a ruling priesthood who wielded tremendous power and influence over Pharaoh. Moses had grown up in Pharaoh's household and naturally was exposed to the occultic powers of the sorcerers.

Black magick gains its power from Satan. When a sorcerer makes a pact with Satan or his demons, those demonic entities agree to serve the sorcerer during his life and to do his bidding. Upon his death, the status is reversed and the sorcerer becomes the servant of his demon. Thus when a person makes this kind of pact, he will do everything possible to prolong his life. When signing a pact in his own blood, a person may be fully convinced he is strong enough to control the demonic powers at his command, but he deceives himself. Very soon he realizes he must turn all his energies to the problem of self-preservation.

The priests in the New Kingdom in Egypt from 1567 to 1089 B.C. became the sole spokesmen for the gods, without whose blessing few enterprises succeeded. The priesthood was the source of a great deal of learning, including writing, astronomy, and the occult, and black magick was the handmaiden of their religion. Sir Wallis Budge, a nineteenth century British Egyptologist, described one occultic practice, a conspiracy against Ramses III about 1200 B.C. A treasury official used wax dolls to attempt to kill the king, but the plot was discovered and defeated. A later Greek tale concerns the Egyptian king Nectanebo II in 350 B.C. He fought battles with these occultic wax figures. As a real enemy marched or sailed against Egyptian forces, Nectanebo would create wax soldiers or ships representing the opposing armies. When the figures fell, so did their real-life counterparts, assuring Egyptian victory.[1]

In Egypt, as everywhere since, spells, incantations, and images were used to perform black magick. The demons knew the words and responded to commands to perform the evil deeds of the priests and sorcerers. The words had power, not in themselves, but because the demons backed them up and performed their destructive assignments.

The book of Exodus describes the confrontation between Moses, Aaron, and Pharaoh. The emissaries of God were asked to perform a miracle to see what sort of spiritual power they had. Aaron threw down his staff, and it became a snake. When Pharaoh summoned his magicians, they were able to perform the same feat. But Aaron's snake swallowed all the Egyptians' snakes!

The sorcerers were also able to duplicate the turning of the Nile into blood and the calling forth of frogs upon the land. When Aaron struck the ground with his staff and turned the dust into gnats, however, they could not produce a similar miracle. They said to Pharaoh, "This is the finger of God." They learned that only God can create life.

The people of Israel had been in Egypt almost four hundred years. They had no Bibles, no places of worship, but only the oral tradition of the God of Abraham, Isaac, and Jacob and His promise of deliverance to a "promised land." After four hundred years of slavery, this promise didn't create much excitement. The religious practices of the Egyptians and the power of black magick were very familiar to the Israelites, and it is likely that many were involved in the occult practices they had learned in Egypt. As they left Egypt, God wanted them to leave behind all such practices and cling to Him alone as their source of power and strength.

The Promised Land

The land of Canaan to which Moses led them was a land steeped in the occult, demonic worship, and demonized people. It is no surprise that God spoke to Moses to warn the people:

> When you enter the land the LORD your God is giving you, do not learn to imitate the detestable ways of the nations there. Let no one be found among you who sacrifices his son or daughter in the fire, who practices divination or sorcery, interprets omens, engages in witchcraft, or casts spells, or who is a medium or spiritist or who consults the dead. Anyone who does these things is detestable to the LORD, and because of these detestable practices the LORD your God will drive out those nations before you. You must be blameless before the LORD your God. The nations you will dispossess listen to those who practice sorcery or divination. But as for you, the LORD your God has not permitted you to do so.
>
> (Deut. 18:9–14)

Sacrifice to demons was a constant temptation for the Israelites. Satan saw that it was a vulnerable spot because of their familiarity with the occult and black magick of Egypt. Having seen its power, there was a tremendous seduction in idolatry, and Canaan provided plenty of opportunity for it. Sadly, the Israelites often succumbed to the temptation, and it resulted ultimately in their downfall.

The Seduction of Israel

The Song of Moses in Deuteronomy 32:17 laments that Israel "sacrificed to demons, not to God." Psalm 106 says,

"They did not destroy the peoples, concerning whom the LORD had commanded them, but they mingled with the Gentiles and learned their works; they served their idols, which became a snare to them. They even sacrificed their sons and their daughters to demons" (v. 34–37).

In Isaiah, we hear the same story:

> But come here,
> You sons of the sorceress,
> You offspring of the adulterer and the harlot!
> Whom do you ridicule?
> Against whom do you make a wide mouth
> And stick out the tongue?
> Are you not children of transgression,
> Offspring of falsehood,
> Inflaming yourselves with gods under every green tree,
> Slaying the children in the valleys,
> Under the clefts of the rocks?
>
> (Isa. 57:3–5)

You can begin to see that Satan was very active in the destruction of the people of Israel through the worship of demons, child sacrifices, witchcraft, and consultations with astrologers, mediums, and spiritists. The Israelites were repeatedly led away by lust and committed sexual sin with male and female temple prostitutes of Baal and Asherah.

The Scripture hints at Satan's organizational structure, a powerful hierarchy of principalities that rule over a people, a city, or a land. In the book of Daniel, we read of Daniel's cry for help and that the angel sent to him was delayed. "But for twenty-one days the mighty Evil Spirit who overrules the kingdom of Persia blocked my way. Then Michael, one of the top officers of the heavenly army, came to help me, so that I was able to break through these spirit rulers of Persia" (Dan. 10:13, TLB).

Perhaps the ruling spirit assigned by Satan over the people of Israel was the spirit of harlotry. "My people ask counsel from their wooden idols, and their staff informs them. For the spirit of harlotry has caused them to stray," says Hosea (4:12), and "the spirit of harlotry is in their midst" (Hos. 5:4).

The power of the evil spirit of harlotry led the people of the ten Northern tribes to their destruction by the Assyrians in 722–721 B.C., and then Jerusalem fell to the Babylonians in 586 B.C.

The final blow to the people of Judah was the evil king Manasseh, who reigned in Jerusalem from 697 to 642 B.C.:

> He did evil in the eyes of the LORD, following the detestable practices of the nations the LORD had driven out before the Israelites. He rebuilt the high places his father Hezekiah had destroyed; he also erected altars to Baal and made an Asherah pole, as Ahab king of Israel had done. He bowed down to all the starry hosts and worshiped them. He built altars in the temple of the LORD . . . to all the starry hosts. He sacrificed his own son in the fire, practiced sorcery and divination, and consulted mediums and spiritists. He did much evil in the eyes of the LORD, provoking him to anger.
>
> (2 Kings 21:2–6)

God's anger was so great that He promised to punish Judah and Jerusalem with the disaster that was the destruction of Jerusalem and the temple of the Lord, and the Babylonian captivity under King Nebuchadnezzar in 587 B.C. Not even the spiritual revival and reforms under King Josiah, who followed Manasseh, could turn away the fierce anger of God because of all that King Manasseh had done. It was too late.

Before we leave the Old Testament, however, we must go back and take a look at Job. Most scholars agree that Job is the oldest book in the Bible, and it gives us some interesting details about Satan. The first chapter of Job describes a conversation between Satan and God. As God reflects on

Job's righteous character, Satan implies that Job obeys God only because God blesses him. "Touch all that he has, and he will surely curse You to Your face!" (v. 11). God gives Satan limited authority over Job, and Satan begins his evil tactics to push Job to the point of cursing God. We see clearly in this passage that Satan is an accuser and the cause of Job's suffering. Satan's work is sickness, suffering, and death. Yet we can also see that Satan is not equal and opposite to God. His power is always under the sovereign authority of God, and, as we shall soon see, was broken by the Son of God, Jesus Christ.

THE COSMIC BATTLE: JESUS AND SATAN

Jesus came on Christmas morn to declare war on Satan, the god of this world. It was an invasion of this planet earth by Jesus to establish the kingdom of God. Probably no one has ever heard a Christmas sermon whose message claimed that the first Christmas was a declaration of war against Satan, but that's exactly what it was.

The purpose of Jesus' birth, according to Galatians 1:4, was a rescue operation: "[He] gave Himself for our sins, that He might deliver us from this present evil age." But there was another purpose as well. "The reason the Son of God appeared was to destroy the devil's work" (1 John 3:8). In 2 Corinthians 4:4 Paul calls Satan the "god of this age," and 1 John 5:19 states that "the whole world is under the control of the evil one." Satan is also described as "the ruler of the kingdom of the air, the spirit who is now at work in those who are disobedient" (Eph. 2:2).

Jesus' purpose in coming here was to destroy Satan and his power over sickness, demons, nature, and death. Christmas was God's "D-Day" on Earth. Yet it didn't take long for Satan to mount a counterattack against the invasion of this planet by the Son of God.

Satan's Counterattack

At the birth of Jesus, magi came from the East seeking the Christ. They asked Herod, "Where is He who has been born King of the Jews? For we have seen His star in the East and have come to worship him" (Matt. 2:2).

Herod was deeply disturbed and asked them to tell him where the baby could be found, claiming that he wanted to worship also. When the magi did not return, he was furious, and, in essence, "put out a contract" to kill all the boys in Bethlehem and the vicinity who were two years old and under. If Joseph had not been warned in a dream to go quickly to Egypt, Jesus could have been killed by Herod's order. Even at His birth there was the shadow of the Cross, and death hung over the manger.

Jesus' Ministry

Through the intervention and protection of the Father, Jesus grew "in wisdom and stature" until He reached manhood. His three years of public ministry began with His baptism by John at the river Jordan. The moment Jesus was baptized, He was filled with the power of God. Immediately Satan attacked Jesus while He was fasting and praying in the wilderness.

The attack was not physical, but he attacked where he thought Jesus would be most vulnerable. Seeing His need for food after forty days of fasting, Satan whispered, "If you are the Son of God, tell these stones to become bread" (Matt. 4:3). Satan often attacks through doubt. Jesus defeated him by quoting the Word of God. "It is written, 'Man shall not live by bread alone, but by every word that proceeds from the mouth of God' " (Matt. 4:4).

Satan's next strategy was aimed at getting Jesus to use His ministry for His own glory and ego needs. "The devil took Him up into the holy city, set Him on the pinnacle of the temple, and said to Him, 'If You are the Son of God, throw

Yourself down. For it is written: "He shall give His angels charge concerning you," and, "In their hands they shall bear you up,/Lest you dash your foot against a stone"'" (Matt. 4:5–6).

Satan was quoting Scripture to Jesus and using doubt to tempt Him. Satan wanted to make Jesus feel a need to prove who He was. But again Jesus answered, "It is written again, 'You shall not tempt the LORD your God'" (v. 7).

Finally, the devil took Jesus to a high mountain and showed Him all the kingdoms of the world and their splendor. "And all this I will give you," he said, "if you will bow down and worship me" (v. 9). The temptation was to have power—power over all the world—if Jesus would only bow down to Satan in worship. But Jesus rebuffed him again, saying, "Away with you, Satan! For it is written, 'You shall worship the LORD your God, and Him only you shall serve'" (v. 10).

After His testing by Satan in the wilderness, Jesus returned to Galilee "in the power of the Spirit" to commence His ministry.

JESUS ON THE OFFENSIVE

Now it was Jesus' turn to take the battle to Satan. When He was handed the scroll of Isaiah to read in the synagogue while visiting His hometown of Nazareth, He read from chapter 61:

> The Spirit of the LORD God is upon Me,
> Because the LORD has anointed Me
> To preach good tidings to the poor;
> He has sent Me to heal the brokenhearted,
> To proclaim liberty to the captives . . .
> To proclaim the acceptable year of the LORD.
> (Isa. 61:1–2; see also Luke 4:18–19)

Then Jesus stunned the people of His town by saying, "Today this Scripture is fulfilled in your hearing!"

Jesus came to destroy the power of Satan in sickness, demon possession, death, and nature, and to set Satan's captives free. He wielded two great weapons in His battle against the kingdom of darkness: exorcism and healing.

Casting Out Demons

Very soon after Jesus began His public ministry, demons began to take notice of Him. In the synagogue at Capernaum one Sabbath, Jesus was teaching when a man possessed by a demon cried out at the top of his voice.

> "Ha! What do you want with us, Jesus of Nazareth? Have you come to destroy us? I know who you are—the Holy One of God!"
>
> "Be quiet!" Jesus said sternly. "Come out of him!" Then the demon threw the man down before them all and came out without injuring him.
>
> (Luke 4:34–35)

The people in the synagogue were amazed at the authority and power of Jesus, a power so great that even evil spirits obeyed Him and left when He gave the order.

Every time a person is set free from demonic bondage, Satan suffers another defeat. It is the kingdom of God present in power. In the twelfth chapter of Matthew, Jesus clearly says that exorcism of demons is the work of the kingdom of God. "If Satan casts out Satan, he is divided against himself. How then will his kingdom stand? . . . But if I cast out demons by the Spirit of God, surely the kingdom of God has come upon you" (vv. 26, 28). The exorcism of demons is proof that the kingdom of God has come among men and is working powerfully.

When Peter preached the good news of Jesus to the household of Cornelius, he said, "You know what has happened throughout Judea, beginning in Galilee after the baptism that John preached—how God anointed Jesus of Nazareth with the Holy Spirit and power, and how he went around doing good and healing all who were under the power of the devil, because God was with him" (Acts 10:37–38). Here we see a bridge to that other powerful weapon Jesus used against Satan's kingdom: healing.

Healing the Sick

Sickness is not the will of God, but is traced to Satan. Jesus did not defy God's will by healing and raising the dead—He affirmed it. Jesus said He came to do the will of the Father who sent Him, and He did only that which He saw the Father doing.

Christians have been confused for years about the source of sickness and death. They have believed they should simply resign themselves to "the will of God" in their suffering. But Jesus demonstrated that sickness and death are of Satan, and He came to break Satan's power. Jesus did not say that all physical sickness is caused by demon possession; He said only that Satan is a destroyer of humankind and as such uses diseases to destroy and kill. There is an element of mysterious, malignant evil in such diseases as cancer and AIDS, and other human sickness as well.

The miracles of healing—whether they are physical, emotional, or a deliverance from the demonic—give us a picture of the awesome love of Abba Father who sent us Jesus, the suffering servant. Jesus healed people and set captives free because people were sick, and His healing words and touch brought forth the love of God as never before. Every time a person was healed or set free, he experienced God's love for him in a very real, life-changing way! As James Kallas so eloquently put it in his book, *The Real Satan,* "Jesus, with the Jews of old, looked at the staggering menace of widespread disease. He did not psychologize or philosophize or seek to explain in medical jargon what was taking place—he healed!"[2]

The last healing act Jesus performed was the most powerful of all. He called Lazarus, dead for four days, to come forth from the tomb! This miracle took place when pilgrims were coming to Jerusalem from all over the world to celebrate the Passover. I would love to have been there to see Lazarus come out of his tomb. Can you imagine how quickly and excitedly the news of this miracle spread through Bethany, just outside of Jerusalem? Throngs of pilgrims and the whole city of Jerusalem were buzzing with the news that Lazarus, dead for four days, was now alive! It is no wonder that when Jesus rode into Jerusalem on Palm Sunday the excited crowd shouted their hosannas as He entered the holy city.

Have you ever wondered how Jesus felt on Palm Sunday? Was He thrilled and excited by the acceptance of the crowd? Did He believe this was the finest hour in His ministry? And when the world collapsed around Him that week—from Judas's betrayal, followed by Peter's denials, the tragic trial, and the crowd demanding His death—did He go to Calvary a disillusioned, depressed, innocent man tragically victimized by Satan?

Jesus' Ultimate Victory: The Cross

I'm sure Satan believed everything that happened to Jesus leading to His death on the Cross was the result of his personal direction and orchestration. When Jesus died, Satan thought he had won.

But Jesus knew well in advance that He was going to the Cross, and it didn't take Him by surprise in the least. At Caesarea Philippi Jesus had begun to explain to His disciples that "He must go to Jerusalem, and suffer many things from the elders and chief priests and scribes, and be killed, and be raised the third day" (Matt. 16:21).

From that point on, as Jesus walked to Jerusalem, He

knew what was ahead of Him and that it was for this purpose He had been born. He knew He must enter into the realm of death to destroy Satan's power over death. "Since the children have flesh and blood, he too shared in their humanity so that by his death he might destroy him who holds the power of death—that is, the devil—and free those who all their lives were held in slavery by their fear of death" (Heb. 2:14–15).

When Jesus rode into Jerusalem on Palm Sunday, He knew He rode there to die. He knew the prophecy of Isaiah 53 would be fulfilled in Him:

> He is despised and rejected by men,
> A Man of sorrows and acquainted with grief.
> And we hid, as it were, our faces from Him;
> He was despised, and we did not esteem Him.
> Surely He has borne our griefs
> And carried our sorrows;
> Yet we esteemed Him stricken,
> Smitten by God, and afflicted.
> But He was wounded for our transgressions,
> He was bruised for our iniquities;
> The chastisement for our peace was upon Him,
> And by His stripes we are healed.
>
> (Isa. 53:3–5)

Jesus knew that the pain of His death would be terrifying, and He cried out in His darkest hour, as foretold in Psalm 22, to His Father, "My God, My God, why have You forsaken Me?"

Yet He was not a helpless victim of the forces of man or Satan that He could not resist. Jesus died not because Pilate was a weak, frightened man. He died not because Judas was a traitor. Jesus died because He intended to die in order to conquer death and Satan's power over death.

Easter was no surprise to Jesus. It was His reason for coming. He came to give His life as the Lamb of God who takes away the sin of the world and our guilt. Jesus came to fulfill the old covenant and to ratify a new one, bringing us salvation through faith in Him, not through works of the law. As the apostle Paul so beautifully writes:

> The righteousness of God . . . is through faith in Jesus Christ, to all and on all who believe. For there is no difference; for all have sinned and fall short of the glory of God, being justified freely by His grace through the redemption that is in Christ Jesus, whom God set forth as a propitiation by His blood, through faith.
>
> > (Rom. 3:22–25)

Jesus is not the victim of Satan. Jesus is victor over Satan. A whole new day began on Easter morning, a victory over death and Satan. The final victory will take place when Christ returns to raise the dead, reward His people, and banish Satan and his followers to eternal suffering and anguish in hell.

The Mystery of the Kingdom

Many people were disappointed in Jesus as the promised Messiah. There was no revolution, no victory over the Romans. There was no sign or word from Jesus about an earthly kingdom like the powerful kingdom of Israel under King David.

And Jesus didn't heal everyone who was sick. He never once looked down from the mountainside, waving His hands as He said to the large crowds gathered below Him, "You will all be healed now!" No, Jesus did the kingdom's work of healing and deliverance one person at a time.

George Eldon Ladd addresses this mysterious "already-but-not-yet" nature of the kingdom:

> The kingdom of God is here, but there is a mystery—a new revelation about the kingdom. Instead of destroying human

sovereignty, it has attacked the sovereignty of Satan. The kingdom of God is here; but instead of making changes in the external political order of things, it is making changes in the spiritual order and in the living men and women.

This is the mystery of the kingdom, the truth which God now discloses for the first time in redemptive history. God's kingdom is yet to come in the form prophesied by Daniel when every human sovereignty will be displaced by God's sovereignty. The world will yet behold the coming of God's kingdom with power. But the mystery, the new revelation, is that this very kingdom of God has now come to work among men but in an utterly unexpected way. It is not now destroying human rule. It has come quietly, unobtrusively, secretly. It can work among men and never be recognized by the crowds. In the spiritual realm, the kingdom now offers to men the blessing of God's rule, delivering them from the power of Satan and sin. The kingdom of God is an offer, a gift which may be accepted or rejected.[3]

A New Confidence

As I searched the Scriptures, the Holy Spirit enabled me to see the panoramic view of the warfare Satan has waged against God and His people since the beginning of time. But I also discovered the tremendous victory won by Jesus and entrusted to the church. I discovered the mandate He has given us to continue the warfare and obtain the victory purchased by Christ.

Dr. Johannes Burgenhagen was the pastor of the Wittenberg Town Church during the time of Martin Luther and, in fact, officiated at Luther's wedding. He wrote a treatise that summarizes perfectly the facts contained in Scripture regarding Satan. Five key truths can be extracted from Burgenhagen's work:

1. The devil is a real, personal, and present entity.
2. He is the "prince" and "god" of this world.
3. He blinds those who do not believe the gospel.

4. Only Christ can defeat him, so do not rely on your own strength and works. Rather, despair completely of your own powers, merits, and of yourself . . . and trust yourself only to Jesus Christ, who is stronger than the devil.
5. In Christ we can withstand and defeat Satan.[4]

I have learned to believe and totally rely on these truths. They have given me the confidence I need as I've faced the threatening evil of the kingdom of darkness.

PART TWO

THE LEFT-HAND PATH

Satan himself masquerades as an angel of
light. It is not surprising then, if his
servants masquerade as servants of
righteousness.

(2 Cor. 11:14–15)

4

SUBTLE SNARES

My people are destroyed for lack of
knowledge.

(Hos. 4:6)

C. S. LEWIS, in his classic book, *The Screwtape Letters,*
cleverly imagines the supposed correspondence between
two devils. The senior devil, Screwtape, is assigned to
teach the finer points of temptation to his younger protegé,
Wormwood. Wormwood has been given a young Christian
and is supposed to lure him away from The Enemy (God)
into Satan's camp. In Lewis's profoundly insightful way,
Screwtape sends the younger demon this advice:

> You will say that these are very small sins; and doubtless,
> like all young tempters, you are most anxious to be able to
> report spectacular wickedness. But do remember the only
> thing that matters is the extent to which you separate the
> man from The Enemy. It does not matter how small the sins
> are, provided that their cumulative effect is to edge the man
> away from the Light and out into the Nothing. Murder is no
> better than cards, if cards can do the trick. Indeed, the
> safest road to Hell is the gradual one—the gentle slope, soft

underfoot, without sudden turnings, without milestones, without signposts.[1]

In precisely this way, gradually and without signposts, many seemingly innocent and harmless pursuits in American life today can become the subtle snares that lead to involvement in the occult and demonic activity. The occult is the "left-hand" path. It is the illegitimate means people use to gain power and the knowledge God prohibits.

Power can come from only two sources: God and Satan. Therefore, that which does not come from God through Christ comes from Satan. The appeal of the occult is an appeal to our curiosity, to our interest in secret and mysterious knowledge and supernatural power. In many cases, we seek supernatural knowledge because we desire to know the future. Our hunger for power represents the wish to gain control, not only over our own lives, but over the lives of others. The occult way encourages us to choose the left-hand path to obtain knowledge and power from a source other than God. This is the same temptation that Satan offered Adam and Eve. You can be like God, he said. You can know everything. (See Gen. 3:5.)

Americans are very naive about the subtle snares that can lead to serious occult involvement and bondage. In their thirst for entertainment, excitement, and unusual experiences, they have invited the demonic realm into their lives and living rooms. Through confusion and ignorance, many have become seriously ensnared. Sadly, the church has not prepared individual Christians to deal with the hidden but very real dangers of the occult.

I was shocked and horrified to hear that Nancy Reagan had been using an astrologist to help make plans for the future, not just for President Reagan, but for the whole country! Both of the Reagans claimed to be "born again" Christians, yet did not see anything wrong with consulting astrologers—a practice the Bible strictly forbids. And the

American people did not appear to be too shocked by the news. Perhaps this is because an estimated 40 million Americans regularly consult their horoscopes with the help of 10,000 professional and 175,000 part-time astrologers. This amounts to a $200,000,000 a year business.[2]

People of our time have openly embraced the occult religions of India and Tibet. Many have somehow come to the conclusion that Eastern religions are more spiritual than Christianity. Gurus have come to America and received a warmer response than they had at home. Courses in yoga abound in health clubs, community centers, schools, and even in churches. Transcendental Meditation (TM) is widely taught to help people reduce stress. But few realize that one goal of TM is to achieve out-of-body experiences that, as we shall see, can leave people open to unwanted demonic visitors.

Perhaps one of the most subtle snares of our day is the lure of fantasy games. Many believe these games are harmless and expect them to lead to enhanced creativity. Who can object to using your imagination for an afternoon or evening of fun? Yet the addictive qualities of these games have led some players into unhealthy obsessions, demonic attacks, and in some cases even murder and suicide.

DUNGEONS AND DRAGONS

The most well known of the fantasy games is Dungeons and Dragons. Although not every person who plays this and other games will become ensnared by them, they have a seductive appeal to many, especially teenagers, who are vulnerable to their dangerous obsessive qualities. With evidence from clinicians and law enforcement professionals, there is a rapidly growing understanding of the tragic harvest that some Dungeons and Dragons players can reap.

Dungeons and Dragons is a complicated game in which each player chooses to assume the identity of an imaginary character. Because characters with evil and violent powers generally score more points and live longer, players tend to claim powers of evil in order to have the best chance of winning. Dwarfs, knights, thieves, gods, and devils, using witchcraft and magic spells, people the game. This game is a journey into a land of fantasy through complicated images. Players use their wits to kill their enemies or be killed, all in the quest for power and wealth. A Dungeon Master orchestrates and referees the game, creating scenarios that are complicated and terrifying. No board is used, only dice.

A Teenage Tragedy

A friend of mine, author Ted Schwarz, showed me the diary of a teenager who committed suicide as the result of his obsession with Dungeons and Dragons. In the Denver area alone, twenty similar stories were reported in the two years following the boy's death.

The young man's name is not important. He might be your son, your brother, your best friend. He was a good student, bright and articulate, the type of young man you expect will go to college, enter a profession, marry and rear a family, and become an asset to the community. When he was fourteen his walls were covered with posters of Cheryl Tiegs wearing the latest swimwear. But then his interest turned to expanding his mind through fantasy games such as Dungeons and Dragons.

Increasingly, he withdrew to his room and closed the door. The games became an obsession. He traded the posters of models for images of mythological monsters and imaginary violent creatures of the night. Although no one realized it at the time, the world of fantasy was becoming his reality, and the boy began sliding gently, almost imperceptibly, into madness.[3]

From his diary we read about the creation of a character who would represent him:

After serious contemplation I have finally entitled myself as Maskim Xul. There is no joy filled laughter in mine ear. No love in mine heart. Just hatred burning hot in my veins. Day after day I pray for the damnation of mankind. And with the coming of night I rejoice in the horrified screams of people as I thrust my hideous weapon into their bodies, tearing them open until they are nothing but a pile of lifeless and bleeding flesh. My gloom. Finding sanctuary in the dark bowels of the earth, I am the beast that growls in pain, and I will avenge myself until my thirst for blood has been appeased. So heed the words, all who may listen. I walk a path that only Metaxul has dared venture. And unless you are he, from this moment on live your life in terror.

But as I grew, evil became more and more a part of my life. I found that I had a definite evil about me. But it went to extremes. For the most part I was extremely good and truthful. I had a good knowledge about life and human nature. At times, though, the evil came out in full force. And when it did, it was almost chaotic.

This evil only came about in times of anger or when I was scared. But it grew, and soon it came out at any time. There was still an imbalance. Good still out-numbered the evil, and I hadn't become aware of it yet. Ignorance made my body a perfect ally for it.

* * *

I, Maskim Xul, was born in the 6th month, in the 6th day, in the year '66. I bear the number of the beast! From the beginning of my existence I lied and stole for my enjoyment. At an early age I planned rape and murder. My mind has always been cluttered with "evil" thoughts, and who is my lofty maker? No one, I say! It is I who hath made me what I am today! And it is I who will decide my fate! So it is this that I profess: tomorrow I will be [more] evil than I was today! And with the coming of each night, my mind will be riddled with chaotic disorder.

The diary goes on to relate one unusual game. A friend called upon Satan to help win the game, and he subsequently won. His winning was a curiosity. "Could Satan be real?" he pondered in his diary. "Satan has no interest in becoming involved with a game of fantasy."

He had to know. If Satan was not a reality, he reasoned, then selling his soul would be only a game. If he was a reality, then perhaps the powers of darkness could change the boy's life and bring him happiness.

He made a pact with Satan, and signed it with his own blood. He began to be obsessed with satanism, occult bookstores, and the darkness of evil.

> Soon I rejected the traditional Catholic goal of God and Jesus Christ. I deny all their prayers and rites. I pledge my allegiance to the Lord Satan and follow along the left-hand path. My morals are gone. I have no feeling for humanity. Each day I pray for the damnation of mankind. My mind and its monstrous thoughts have become inhuman. Sanity is not the question. I am as sane as the next, though my views reap great harm in the minds of others. My cause is known. I do not claim to be as the next for I am one of a kind. My decayed mind will forever be riddled with evil. But I am reality.

After two years of involvement with Dungeons and Dragons he felt his death was very near. The last entry in his diary contains these words:

> Upon reading these words you will know that I am dead. I have now started the lonesome journey to the bowels of the earth. I travel the twisted road that winds its way down to the forsaken pit. It is time to meet my lofty maker! My destination will be the foot of the throne where I will kneel and greet my father. Thus ending my travel wearily I will scale the great monument and seat myself by the side of my lord, bowing my head in shame for I had not the strength nor the courage to continue my earthly existence. Though I am a shameful sight, my father will spread his wings and welcome me to his and my real home. . . . My death is one

that could have been avoided. I could have lived for a long time here with you. . . . But something went wrong. My senses began to sharpen rapidly and to live became a discomfort. I was caught between the hatred for this world and the thirst for blood. My plight for evil became stagnant. The only instinct was to act and act fast, so ending my life.

After he finished this entry, he went to the garage, closed the door, and started a car's engine. His mother was grocery shopping and would not return for at least an hour, and his father was at work. By the time the youth was discovered, the carbon monoxide had done its work; the boy was dead.

The problem for this bright young man was more than just a psychological obsession. I believe that when he took the left-hand path to the occult and Satan, he opened the door of his life and, in essence, invited demons to come in. His pact with Satan was not a game, but a bondage culminating in the highest form of worship to Satan—suicide.

Parents Fighting Back

Patrica Pulling founded a group called BADD, Bothered About Dungeons and Dragons, in Richmond, Virginia, when her sixteen-year-old son committed suicide after playing Dungeons and Dragons in school.

Dungeons and Dragons was explored on a "60 Minutes" segment that aired in September 1985. Host Ed Bradley described Pat and Lee Pulling returning home three years earlier to find their son, Bink, dead on the front lawn. He had put a bullet in his heart with his father's handgun. Until that night the Pullings had never heard of the game Dungeons and Dragons. Then they began looking through Bink's things:

We went into the kitchen, and there on the table were what we thought were just regular composition books with schoolwork in them. Instead they were filled with Dungeons and Dragons material along with this curse he had received in the game that day before he died. The curse which was placed on Bink's Dungeons and Dragons character began, "Your soul is mine. I choose the time." In a letter that he left, Bink said he had been summoned to kill himself because he was evil.[4]

"It was obvious through his writing," said Pat Pulling, "that he felt he had assumed this character, but what I couldn't get into my mind was, is it possible? How could anybody do that? How could a sixteen-year-old who is smart, intelligent—why would he believe that he was something in a game and why would he kill himself because somebody else said to do it? Bink was well adjusted . . . he never had psychological problems. He was healthy, even physically healthy."[5]

Another guest on the "60 Minutes" show was psychiatrist Thomas Radecky, a professor at the University of Illinois Medical School and chairman of the National Coalition on Television Violence. He had studied the effects of the game for several years and related that there had been, up to that time, twenty-eight deaths related to Dungeons and Dragons.

Dr. Radecky said:

> In some of those, [the game] was clearly the decisive element. In other ones, it was just a major element in the thinking of the people at the time they committed suicide or murder. It's not coincidence, not when you have careful documentation, you have careful notes, you have eyewitnesses. For instance, in one case the parents actually saw their child summon Dungeons and Dragons' demons into his room before he killed himself. In another case the child had thought he had the ability to astral travel coming from the Dungeons and Dragons game. He thought that he could leave his body and come back, and he had rigged it up just according to the rule book so he could do it. He was sur-

rounded by his materials, and put a bullet in his head so he could leave his body, and he's never come back.[6]

A Case of Murder

In the Oklahoma State Penitentiary the youngest death-row inmate is a sixteen-year-old who was convicted of murder. Sean Sellers is an intense, intelligent loner who went from being a twelve-year-old absorbed in playing Dungeons and Dragons to a Satan worshiper who then killed his parents. A year before she was murdered, Mrs. Sellers took Sean to a clergyman to discuss his fascination with satanism.

"We hear this all the time," Patricia Pulling says. "A mother even had her child in a psychiatric institution and the therapist kept saying, 'Don't worry about it, it's just a fad.' This kid was doing satanic rituals on her dining room table."[7]

Satan is very clever in deceiving people and tempting them with "goodies" if they will start down the left-hand path. The game Dungeons and Dragons is touted as a way to enhance creative thought, and even some schools are using it to stimulate the imagination. But there is no warning, "Danger! Playing this game may result in demonic possession and death!"

THE OCCULT: THE LURE OF KNOWLEDGE

The apostle Paul warned, "The god of this age has blinded the minds of unbelievers, so that they cannot see the light of the gospel of the glory of Christ" (2 Cor. 4:4). Unfortunately, the god of this age has also blinded the minds of many believers as well. You would be surprised how many of your family, friends, and fellow church members have been or are involved in occult practices. Most don't understand what is wrong with what they are doing.

Some of the more common occult practices include astrology, channeling, tarot cards, healing crystals, seances, seeking the advice of psychics, palm reading, tea leaves, automatic writing, past life regression through hypnosis, astral travel, mind control, fortune telling, EST, witchcraft (white, gray, or black), *I Ching,* numerology, Ouija boards, transcendental meditation and yoga, pendulum healing, voodoo, spiritualism, and the New Age.

While much of modern Christianity in the West is being despiritualized and becoming more intellectual and rational, there is a deep hunger in people for the spiritual and supernatural. People are seeking spiritual answers and meaning for their lives. The occult offers an answer to the need for the transcendent, the mysterious, and the forbidden.

It is a paradox that in our scientific age, with the glorification of the rational mind, there is a corresponding rise in interest in the supernatural, or nonrational world. The word *occult* refers to knowledge and power beyond the boundary of normal intellectual knowledge. It is derived from the Latin word *occultus* meaning "hidden, secret, dark, mysterious, concealed." It is used to describe phenomena that transcend the world of the five senses.[8]

Dr. Kurt Koch, a Lutheran pastor in Germany, spent forty years counseling over twenty thousand people who were involved in the occult. A prolific writer on the subject, he states in his book *Occult Bondage and Deliverance:*

> Historically speaking, the rules of occultism have remained unchanged throughout all the different epochs of man. The actual practices of occultism are the same today as they were 5,000 years ago. Second to this is the fact that no matter what the evil of civilization, the methods used by that civilization remain the same. The form may change but the underlying principles remain unchanged.
>
> Suffice it to say that the Shaman Alualak, whom I met in

Alaska, used the same methods and the same powers in his occult practices as his colleagues in the tropical heat of the Amazon jungles. They differed but in name, for in the men of the Amazon they are called the Kahontschi. In Jamaica they are called Obiahs, in Bali, Indonesia, the Dukunonba-han. On Hawaii the black magicians call themselves the Ka-huna, and on the Fiji Islands, the Drunikau. In spite of their racial, linguistic, geographical and cultural differences, all of these are skilled in the same art.[9]

Thus we see that, despite their outward forms, occult practices are timeless, and they deal with essentially the same aims and motives: the lust for knowledge and the lust for power.

Astrology

Astrology was developed in ancient Babylonia as the art of foretelling the future from the juxtaposition of the sun, moon, and planets. Despite its ancient roots, it has never been more popular than it is in American culture today. Newspapers across the country carry daily horoscopes, which many otherwise intelligent people rely on to plan their days. Often people view this as a harmless activity, but in reality it is a subtle, deceptive invitation to walk the left-hand path of the occult.

What is the danger of astrology? First, it is idolatry be-cause it seeks knowledge from a source other than God. Second, it provides false and deceptive knowledge that of-ten leads people astray. The prophet Isaiah ridiculed the as-trologers and their impotence to save or direct the people:

> Let now the astrologers, the stargazers,
> And the monthly prognosticators
> Stand up and save you
> From what shall come upon you.
> Behold, they shall be as stubble,
> The fire shall burn them;

They shall not deliver themselves
From the power of the flame.

              (Isa. 47:13–14)

Fortune Telling

The desire to know the future has driven people to seek knowledge from palm reading, tarot cards, crystal balls, and fortune tellers. The practitioners of these occult arts have often had the reputation of being charlatans and frauds. Somehow, though, it hasn't stopped people from seeking their advice. Today we see a new type of fortune teller: the psychic. These occultists charge up to $250 or $300 an hour for making predictions. The source of their knowledge is "channeling," through which they lend their bodies and voices to spirit entities who speak through them. Although the entities sometimes pose as interplanetary visitors or departed spirits, they are in fact nothing more than demons. It amazes me that people pay good money to receive the advice of a demonic spirit! It is just as the apostle Paul predicted, "The Spirit expressly says that in latter times some will depart from the faith, giving heed to deceiving spirits and doctrines of demons" (1 Tim. 4:1).

Ouija Board

The Ouija board is another means of obtaining supernatural knowledge. Isaac Fuld, who patented the Ouija board in 1892, stated on his application that the planchette (the pointing device on which people place their fingers) was moved by a spirit force. Any time a person invites a spirit to communicate with him, he is leaving himself wide open to demon activity. This "game" has outsold the game of Monopoly.[10]

I once talked with a very worried mother, who was concerned about her fourteen-year-old daughter, Jane. Jane and her best friend had been playing with a Ouija board for about three months. Jane was fascinated with the occult and had been studying astrology and wanted to be a white witch. About three weeks earlier, she had come to her mother looking very frightened. "The devil has taken over my soul and wants me to commit suicide," she declared. Jane showed her mother several pieces of paper containing words she said were from a demon writing through her. In shaky script, not Jane's normal handwriting, they said:

> You are bad. Be evil to God. I am bad. I lie and make you draw weird pictures. You should run away and come to be with me because you are evil like me. You are stubborn and you are going to die very soon. You are evil, evil, and you are going to hell. I don't think you will survive very much longer. I have been working on you for too long. I make you bleed inside. I hate you. I hate you. You are evil. Kill yourself before Dad does. You will die. It's bad, isn't it. Kill yourself now or I will kill you. Kill yourself. Kill. Kill.

Jane's mother was shaken. She had difficulty believing in demons, yet it seemed the only explanation. A few days later she brought her daughter in for deliverance, and Jane was gloriously set free.

The use of Ouija boards is one of the easiest ways to open yourself up and invite the presence of demons. Ed and Lorraine Warren, who have the unusual title "demonologists," study demon activity in people and houses, as in *The Amityville Horror.* Ed Warren says:

> Of the cases we respond to, four in ten concern individuals who have raised inhuman spirits using a Ouija board. The Ouija board is nothing by itself. It's just a pressed piece of board with the alphabet on it. The same effect can be had with an upside down wine glass on a waxed table. In other words, it's what you use the object for. When you use the Ouija board, you give permission for any unknown spirit to communicate with you. Would you open the front door to your house and let in just anybody? Of course not. Yet that's exactly what you're doing on a supernatural level.[11]

Seances

In Deuteronomy 18:11 the people of Israel are warned not to consult someone "who is a medium or spiritist, or who consults the dead." The desire to communicate with the spirit of a deceased person is especially tempting during the period of grief after the death of a loved one. Again, it can open the door to the spirit world of the demonic. If communication is established with a spirit from the dead, it is a disguised demon, who has access to all the information available about the deceased person.

Seances have sometimes been conducted as a "sucker's game" which fraudulently takes advantage of people and obtains their money with special equipment and stage tricks. I have conducted mock seances for youth groups in which I effectively fooled the young people, then showed them how they were deceived and discussed why they should not attend seances.

The philosopher Wundt once said, "Great minds must have turned into imbeciles on their passing into eternity, because when they are consulted by mediums, the things they say are so dull and trivial."[12] Wundt implies that the mediums were really only producing their own thoughts when great minds of the past were supposedly speaking through them.

I remember how well respected and admired Bishop James A. Pike was until he turned to journey down the left-hand path. Grieving the loss of his son, Bishop Pike sought to contact him through the services of a medium. In his book *The Other Side*, he writes about a seance with medium Eva Twigg. The bishop asked, "Have you heard anything over there about Jesus or a Jesus?"

A spirit, who claimed to be his son, Jim, Jr., spoke through the medium:

> "Oh, it is difficult. I'm afraid I might hurt you. I might hurt you. They talk about him—a mystic, a seer. Yes, a seer. Oh, but Dad, they don't talk about him as a savior. As an

example, you see? You see, I want to tell you. I would like to tell you, Jesus is triumphant, you know? But it's not like that. I don't understand it yet. I may; some time I may. You don't want me to tell you what I don't know—not a savior—that's the important thing—an example. Don't you ever believe that God can be personalized. He is the Central Force, and you all give your quota toward it. Do you agree with me, Dad?"[13]

Bishop Pike believed what he heard from that spirit. He did not heed the words of the apostle John, who warned: "Do not believe every spirit, but test the spirits whether they are of God. . . . By this you know the Spirit of God: Every spirit that confesses that Jesus Christ has come in the flesh is of God, and every spirit that does not confess that Jesus Christ has come in the flesh is not of God. And this is the spirit of the Antichrist, which you have heard was coming, and is now already in the world" (1 John 4:1–3). Ignoring these words, Bishop Pike turned down the left-hand path, and many people were deceived and followed him.

Reincarnation

Another ancient concept experiencing a wave of popularity is the belief in reincarnation. The essence of the doctrine is that each of us has successive lives through which we work toward perfection. If you are evil in one life, you may be reborn on a lower plane, as an animal, for example; if you are good, you may advance to a higher level in the next life. The goal is to make progress during each life and eventually achieve "nirvana," a state of union with all creation but a loss of individual existence—in essence, a state of nothingness.

Hypnotists have made a tremendous amount of money from this belief in reincarnation. Using "hypnotic regression," they attempt to put their clients in touch with their former lives. The danger in hypnosis is that individuals allow themselves to be placed in a passive state. During this very vulnerable and passive time, it is much easier for demons to gain access to them, provide detailed information about supposed previous lives, and lead them one step closer to bondage and deception.

Reincarnation is an enticing belief, because it allows people to avoid judgment for their wrong actions. It provides unlimited second chances. However, it is totally unscriptural. Hebrews 9:27 clearly states, "Man is destined to die once and after that to face judgment." Reincarnation suggests a salvation by works rather than by faith and the free grace of God.

The New Age

Reincarnation is a central feature of the "new spirituality" being proclaimed by members of the New Age movement. Actress Shirley MacLaine focused national attention on New Age philosophy with her book *Out on a Limb,*[14] which became a television movie in 1987. She describes mystical experiences, contact with departed spirits, channeling energy from the "God force," and astral travel (the experience of the soul leaving the body).

The New Age expresses a concern for ecology, world peace, elimination of hunger, nuclear disarmament, positive thinking, crystals and pyramid power, holistic healing, and a positive self-image. It is a collage of old and new thinking that has something to offer just about everyone.

For the majority of people involved in New Age pursuits, I believe it is just a fad. Many of the followers are naive concerning the theology that underlies the movement, or the dangers of occult involvement that lurk there.

The New Age teaches that all religious practices and beliefs are equally true, no matter how different or contradictory they are. It is like the old notion that it doesn't matter what you believe as long as you're sincere. After all, they say, all paths lead to heaven.

A modern-day repackaging of Hinduism, New Age believes that everyone is potentially a god. And therein lies its appeal. It is the old self-centered desire to be as gods with which Satan first tempted humankind in the garden of Eden.

Texe Marrs, in his book *Dark Secrets of the New Age,* outlines eight spiritual falsehoods taught by New Age:

1. A personal god does not exist.
2. Jesus is not the only begotten Son of God and is not the only Christ.
3. Jesus did not die for our sins.
4. There are no such things as sin and evil.
5. There is no Trinity of the Father, Son, and Holy Spirit.
6. The Bible is filled with errors.
7. There is no heaven and no hell.
8. Every man is God and one's godhood can be realized through attainment of a higher consciousness.[15]

This theology reveals that Satan is the spirit behind New Age. He has found one more means by which to oppose God's truth. The movement speaks boldly of communicating with spirits and having spirits enter human beings. Naturally, they do not identify these "spirit guides" as demons, but call them "inner guides," "light bearers," "entities," or "spirits of the great masters." I have worked with people who believed their spirit guides were good for them, only to find that when they turned to Christ, their former guides tried violently to harm them. Once again, Satan had laid a subtle snare beneath an innocent-looking surface in order to catch his prey.

Psychic Healing

I received a letter a few years ago from a dentist who had attended one of my seminars. A Christian, he had been deceived into becoming involved with occult practices through the influence of a psychic healer. He wrote:

Having been raised Catholic, I felt very close to God; He was and is the center of my life. I married a great girl who felt the same way I did about God. We had five beautiful children.

In 1968 I met a psychic healer who eventually lived with us. We got into meditation, auras, astrology, numerology, trance states, hypnosis—you name it, we experienced it all. Our psychic friend could do things that made Edgar Cayce look small time. . . . I opened a holistic health center and we had our share of nice healings. There soon were over 20 professionals involved over a period of 3–1/2 years.

Behind the scenes, though, my marriage was destroyed, the kids got into the drug scene, and two of our daughters had babies out of wedlock. Those people who were involved with us were having lots of divorces and separations. The holistic health center became a financial disaster and because of the overwhelming debt, I had to close it. All this nearly destroyed me.

During this time we learned a great many principles of truth that worked, but I also bought into reincarnation and the theory that a lot of the problems were because we were "working out of karma."

The prince of darkness comes as an angel of light and shows us lots of truth (about 95 percent). The 5 percent that wasn't truth was the hook in the bait that caused me to relate to Jesus Christ in a different way, and set me up to work with power that wasn't all of Jesus. I "saw" all the power as coming from God.

Finally, a vision of Jesus given to a close friend warned us that "by their fruits you will know them." After several years of Bible study and an intensive effort to focus on *Jesus* and *detach* myself from occult strings attached to me, I am feeling and experiencing the joy of being more totally in Jesus Christ. It was hard and the strings are so subtle, it is difficult to see them unless Christ is the constant focus!

The snare of psychic healing is that it appears so good and praiseworthy on the surface. Who can argue with efforts to alleviate pain and sickness? Satan has the power to heal, and this seduction is very strong because it is supernatural. Modern Western Christianity basically has turned its back on divine healing through the power of the Holy Spirit, so that void has left a door open for demonic powers of healing to lead people down the left-hand path.

I once met a Christian man who lived for three years among psychic healers in the Philippines. He was the personal guide for one of the healers in a tour across the United States. He studied with these healers and believed them to be Christians. They had extensive knowledge of the Bible and preached like Christian evangelists. But he discovered he had been deceived because the source of the healing power was not of God. The foundation of their belief was spiritism, and the source of the healing power was demonic. He returned to the Philippines and confronted the psychic healers; then he revisited every city and group he had conducted the healer to, confessed his sin, and asked forgiveness.

Johanna Michaelson worked for fourteen months with a psychic healer in Mexico. A seeker after God, she became very deeply involved in mind control and yoga, and assisted a psychic healer named Pachitas. She was given two spirit guides, Jesus and Mamacita, to teach her in deep meditation. Later on, Johanna was led to confront her spirit guides:

> "You are not the Jesus of the Bible, are you?" I challenged the figure of "Jesus" which stood before me in the shadows. There was no reply. His eyes were closed. Mamacita stood close by him. "Then I command you, in the name of Jesus Christ of Nazareth, tell me: Do you believe that Jesus Christ is God uniquely incarnate in human flesh?" A violent flash as though from a powerful bomb brought the walls of my amethyst and gold laboratory down all around me. When I looked up, my counselors had vanished. Again,

I looked at the words of Deuteronomy and Leviticus. The questions were finally settled. The works of a medium were abominations before God. Neither the psychic perceptions of mind control nor Pachitas' work had its source in God.[16]

The Left-Hand Path

The left-hand path of the occult, no matter how innocent it looks on the surface, is one of deception and evil. At first glance, many occult practices appear to be harmless parlor games, especially to the person who doesn't have a belief system that includes the spiritual reality of God and Satan. When I think of the easy grade of the left-hand path, I can't help remembering the insightful words of C. S. Lewis, who seemed to perfectly describe the slow descent into destruction: "Indeed, the safest road to hell is the gradual one—the gentle slope, soft underfoot, without sudden turning, without milestones, without signposts."[17]

Satan doesn't care whether it is small steps or giant steps that take us in his direction, so long as that is where we are headed.

5

WITCHCRAFT: THE LUST FOR POWER

Let no one be found among you who . . .
engages in witchcraft, or casts spells.

(Deut. 18:10–11)

THE SEDUCTIVE LURE of the occult is twofold: the promise of knowledge and the promise of power. Enticing promises that you can discover "ancient wisdom" and "the secrets of the masters" are coupled with assurances by occult practitioners that you can know the future. In Chapter 4 we looked at many of the forms of occultism that seek forbidden knowledge such as astrology and other forms of fortune telling, the Ouija board, and seances. There are different levels of involvement in these practices, from surface dabbling to heavy dependence. If warned at an early stage, people involved with these things can still renounce them and free themselves from any resulting demonic influences.

But getting free is much more difficult for those involved in a deeper level of occultism—the lust for power, which is most clearly manifested in the practice of witchcraft. This practice does not merely seek illicit knowledge, for the main objective is having the power to use illicit knowledge to control other people's lives.

Witchcraft has made tremendous gains in popularity in America because it has been portrayed as rather harmless. One article in *The Arizona Republic,* entitled "A Pox on You," reveals the latest fad in witchcraft.

> Well, my friends, things are getting curiouser and curiouser. We not only live in an age where we lay out two bucks, dial a "976" number and hear jokes, our horoscopes, or dirty talk; we live in an age where we can dial and cast a love spell or curse an enemy. That's right, boys and girls, dial 976-SPEL in some cities and poof! A pox on you!
>
> There are 10 spells for love and prosperity. There are 31 curses available to bring bad luck to a victim. The spells are very spooky sounding—peppered with a lot of maniacal laughter—and, according to the witches I know, they are . . . ritualistically correct.[1]

The history of witchcraft from ancient times to the present is long and complicated. The media most often report on the "white witchcraft" that appears very rarely in the witch legends of the past. White witches claim they are not sorcerers, satanists, or Christians. They practice "good" magic for healing people and causing good things to happen.

WHITE WITCHCRAFT

Modern white witches claim to be heirs to an unbroken religious tradition stretching back into primeval history. They worship the Great Mother, the earth mother, the symbol of fertility and the oldest and most elemental of the ancient gods. White witchcraft insists that it is a religion and not an evil cult.[2]

White witches draw a distinction between white magick and black magick. But the source of power for white witchcraft, or white magick, is the same as that of black magick: it is demonic. Remember, any supernatural power that is not of God is of Satan.

The Modern Witch of Wicca

Wicca is the contemporary name for the cult of neo-paganism, or white witchcraft. It has been flourishing in the west and especially in the central United States since the 1960s. Wicca believers state categorically that their "old religion" is not involved in Satan worship. The religion of Wicca is supposed to be older than Christianity. The gods of Wicca are a Mother Goddess who ruled the earth, the moon, the sea, and things of agriculture, and the Harvest God who ruled fishing and hunting.

William Schnoebelen, a former high priest in Wicca, explains that there are many differences between Wicca groups. In his book *Wicca: Satan's Little White Lie,* he describes some of the variations he found. For example, some groups perform their ceremonies nude, while others wear robes. In some groups members are scourged with a whip during a ceremony, but most groups do not use whips. Some groups practice ritual sex and sexual orgies; others abstain from sexual ceremonies.

There are, however, a few common elements in all Wicca and neo-paganist practices:[3]

- A polytheistic worldview with usually a god/goddess pair
- A belief in Westernized reincarnation, which does not believe in moving back to be reincarnated as animals, but only forward to be reborn as humans
- A shamanistic worldview similar to animism, in which objects have lives and souls
- Militant feminism and politically left-wing philosophies

- A do-your-own-thing morality as long as it "doesn't hurt anyone else"
- A view of human destiny that believes people can evolve spiritually through their own efforts and ultimately attain either enlightenment or godhood

Links to Satanism

The writings of Gerald Gardner and his book of witchcraft rituals, entitled the *Book of Shadows,*[4] play an important part in Wicca. There is a real controversy in the organization about the possible link between Gardner and a leading satanist of this century, Aleister Crowley. Some have suggested that Gardner commissioned Crowley to write parts of the *Book of Shadows.* Crowley, who died in 1947, once boasted that he was "the wickedest man in the world." He was a black magick practitioner and took part in ceremonial satanic sex rituals. Two leading historians of contemporary Wicca, Doreen Valiente and Margot Adler, have both found connections between the writing of the *Book of Shadows* and Crowley.[5]

Renowned leaders in Wicca, such as Sybil Leek, the author of *Diary of a Witch,* and Alex Sanders, are also linked to Aleister Crowley. Leek studied under Crowley and said that he had a profound influence on her life. She also claimed that his "mantle" was passed on to her. Alex Sanders, one of the most influential people in Wicca, also reported he knew Crowley and studied under him.

William Schnoebelen remarks: "If Wiccans aren't Satanists, why do two of their prominent spokespeople take such pains to associate themselves with the century's leading Satanist?"[6] Schnoebelen, who was a high priest in Wicca until his conversion to Christianity, further writes:

> I'd realized that Wicca, the religion our disciples were following, was just a slightly sanitized version of continental Satan-worship! We still taught them that it was just a

charming little nature cult with herbs and circles and whips, but we knew better. We knew real wisdom came from Satan! It became clear to me that witchcraft was rather like an onion or an artichoke. You had layer upon layer of meaning and secrets.[7]

Schnoebelen described how he began his studies with Wicca, thinking he was doing good and that the rites and ceremonies he participated in were for the benefit of humanity. But soon he began to hunger for more.

In my own personal development as a witch, and the development of almost all our colleagues, I found that after about five or six years it was necessary to begin pursuing the study of the "higher wisdom of Satan" in order to keep growing. Magick is like a drug. You keep needing more in order to stay at the same level at which you feel fulfilled. There is no end to it.[8]

The most well-known satanist in the United States, Anton La Vey, states that "people trying to label themselves as white or gray witches are hiding behind false pride and hypocrisy."[9] If even the head of satanism refuses to divorce white witchcraft from its darker counterparts, why should we? Clearly, attempts to make any kind of witchcraft look "white" are no more than a whitewash!

THE DARKER WORLD OF WITCHCRAFT

Historians date witchcraft back to the Babylonian and Assyrian cultures, but I suspect its power has been in existence from the early days of man. The need for supernatural power has always been a part of humans' history, and it remains with us in both primitive and technologically advanced cultures around the world. The witch doctor of the aborigines in Australia uses black magick. El Curadero, the

Healer of Puerto Rico, does the same. When a Christian pastor asked an Alaskan shaman whose power he used to heal people and even raise them from the dead, he replied, "The power of the devil, of course."[10]

On a visit to Australia, my wife and I heard an expert on the culture of the aborigines state that when a witch doctor "points the bone" to place a curse on someone, it is effective for up to one hundred miles in killing the person at whom the bone was pointed. Even in the popular movie *Crocodile Dundee,* the hero demonstrates his power of black magick learned from the aborigines.

Witchcraft was known in early biblical times. Of Queen Jezebel, Scripture says, "How can there be peace . . . as long as all the idolatry and witchcraft of your mother Jezebel abound?" (2 Kings 9:22). And the Lord spoke through the prophet Micah, saying, "I will destroy your witchcraft and you will no longer cast spells" (Micah 5:12).

Witchcraft flourished in the Middle Ages in Europe, and many current well-known practices have European roots. In 1484 Pope Innocent VIII issued a Papal Bull declaring that witchcraft in all its aspects and practices was heresy. But, although it was strictly forbidden, the church was never able to obliterate it completely. The witchcraft from the Middle Ages and the sixteenth and seventeenth centuries has survived to the present day, and it is currently experiencing a revival in the United States.

Becoming a Witch

Francesco Maria Guazza, a seventeenth-century demonologist, described a ritual for becoming a witch:[11]

- A spoken denial of the Christian faith
- Rebaptism in the devil's name, at which point the novice receives a new name in place of his Christian one
- Symbolic removal of the baptismal chrism (consecrated oil mixed with balm) by the devil's touch

- Denial of godparents and assignment of new sponsors
- Gift of a piece of clothing to the devil as a token of submission
- Oath of allegiance to the devil made while standing in a magic circle
- Inclusion of the initiate's name in the *Book of Death*
- A promise to sacrifice children to the devil
- A promise to pay annual tribute to the devil, such as black-colored gifts
- Marking the initiate with the devil's mark—a strangely shaped area on the skin that becomes insensitive
- Various vows of special service to the devil, including destruction of holy relics and, especially, keeping the secrets of the Sabbath

Festivals

European folklore tells of two major festivals for witches—April 30, the grand sabbat, known as Walpurgis Night, and October 31, All Hallow's Eve. Known today as Halloween, the latter is the night when, according to witchcraft, the barriers between the worlds of life and death are thin as veils, allowing the dead to walk among the living. During these two major festivals, witches gather in great numbers to form a congregation or, as they call it, a coven.

Witches normally meet monthly during the full moon in local covens of thirteen people. The number at meetings may vary, however, from as few as five witches to as many as several thousand. These meetings are called "sabbats."

The Witches' Circle

At the sabbat a circle nine feet in diameter is drawn on the ground or floor using a ritual knife called the "athame." Within the circle is a five-pointed star known as a "pentagram." Tools denoting the elements—earth, air, fire, and water—are placed on an altar. A high priestess conducts special rituals and, while standing in the circle, invokes demons to materialize. At a major annual sabbat, she will ask Satan to appear. An animal, often a goat, is sacrificed. The witches then proceed to a feast that includes drinking wine and strong liquor.

When the feasting is over, the witches begin to dance, sing, and chant. Some dance with broomsticks in commemoration of an ancient fertility rite. As the dancing becomes more uninhibited and a high state of excitement bordering on hysteria or a trance state is achieved, a sexual orgy follows. At major annual sabbats, according to claims, Satan himself materializes and engages in intercourse with the witches. Women who reportedly have had intercourse with Satan insist that it is a very harsh, painful experience. They submitted to it because it represented an affirmation of the evil bond between them.[12]

It is hard for modern educated people to conceive, much less believe, that demons materialize at these sexual orgies, taking on the form of a man or woman for the purpose of engaging in sexual relations with humans. The demonic seducers or rapists of women are called "incubi." The spirits of lust sent to men are named "succubi." Historically the purpose of these demons has been to lead people into sexual sin.[13]

In my experience as an exorcist, I have cast out the power of demons of incubi from women who were sexually assaulted as children during a satanic ritual or who, as adults, had been satanists and were involved in sexual orgies. I have learned not to think of these things as fictional or mythical, because I have seen firsthand the *fact* of satanic bondage and the way it destroys people's lives.

SANTERIA: WITCHCRAFT'S OTHER VERSION

Although witchcraft in the Western world has focused primarily on its European roots, there is a large body of witchcraft that bears no resemblance to the European version. It is called "Santeria," which in Spanish means "worship of the saints." It is the name given to an Afro-Cuban religion that is a mixture of mythology, black magick, and the religious practices of the Yorubas of southwestern Nigeria.

The Yoruba people were sold as slaves and sent to Cuba and Brazil. Since Spanish law decreed that slaves be baptized as Roman Catholics, the Yoruba were forced to give up their religion and become Catholic, at least on the surface. Resistant to this new religion, these slaves hid their gods under the guise of the Catholic saints. For example, when slave owners saw the Yoruba people kneeling and worshiping Our Lady of Mercy, they did not realize the Africans were in reality worshiping their god Orisha Obatala. In the same way, Saint Barbara represented Chango, the god of thunder and fire. Saint Anthony represented Eleggua, the mischievous messenger and trickster. And Saint Lazarus, the patron saint of the sick, became the god Babalu-Age, who could heal or cause diseases.

Saint Peter was the Yoruba god Oggun, the ironworker and patron of all metals. Saint Francis of Assissi was the god Orunla, the diviner of orishas and owner of the table of Ifa—the major divination system of Santeria.

Once slave owners began to realize their mistake, the Santeria religion was persecuted and driven underground, where it was shrouded in secrecy.[14]

Santeria Today

In Cuba today, the Castro government does not recognize any religion except Catholicism, with the exception of Abaqua Santeria. Because Castro does not want to offend the Abaqun people, their priests, or their gods, he has kept his hands off the Montanza area in central Cuba where Santeria is strongest. During the boat lift from Cuba to Florida in 1980, many of the Cubans Castro expelled and sent to us were Santerias of the Abaqua sect.

In 1978 in Havana, a legitimate play was staged, entitled *Abaqua,* which explained all the workings of the secret society. This exposure of the secret rituals and rites resulted in violent retaliation. Within two weeks of the play's opening, all the members of the cast—some twenty people—were killed.[15]

In stores called "botanicas," worshipers can buy items for religious practices, for example, candles, beads, herbs, oils, cauldrons, holy stones, crocks, and plaster statues of Catholic saints. Everything in a botanica is color and number coded to the gods of Santeria or Orishas. A botanica also sells Bibles, rosaries, prayer books, and medals of saints.[16]

The influence of the Yoruba religion has resulted in the birth of offshoot sects called Candombie, Umbanda, and Palo Mayombe. These sects have further developed the dark side of Santeria magick, involving curses, spells, and human sacrifice. In Haiti, Yoruba traditions blended with those of the Fon people of Dahomey and resulted in the birth of voodoo.

Ache and Ebbo: Power and Sacrifice

As in the old Yoruba tradition, Santeria was based on concepts of "Ache," a Yoruba word for divine power, or the power of the god who created the universe. The gods of Santeria, the Orishas, are filled with this power. All the invocations, spells, and rituals are conducted to acquire power, or "ache," from the Orishas or gods. With this spiritual power, all problems can be solved, enemies defeated, and love and money acquired.[17] "Ebbo" is the concept of sacrifice in which the gods of the Santeria are propitiated, so that these gods will give the believers their spiritual power. Therefore, all the spells of Santeria witchcraft are based on this ebbo belief.

Sacrifice, or ebbo, does not always require a sacrificial victim, although animal sacrifice is often used. Ebbo can be an offering of fruits, flowers, candles, or any of the favorite foods of the Orishas. When blood is called for in a sacrifice, great forces are invariably at play, and often a person's life is in danger or some major undertaking is involved.[18]

Santeria has a strong emphasis on ancestor worship. The dead in one's family must be honored and periodically fed. This religion recognizes a direct contact between humans and spirit entities, or gods, for the purpose of receiving spiritual power.

Initiation into Santeria

To enter Santeria, an initiate is taught the mysteries of the cult by a person who becomes the godfather, the *padrino,* or godmother, the *madrina.* The initiate is then encouraged to increase his knowledge of the rituals, secrets, and spiritual power. A *santero,* male, or *santera,* female, takes the name of the god Orisha, in whose mysteries he or she has been initiated. The high priest of Santeria, known as the "Babalawo," conducts sacrifices during initiation ceremonies, confers with certain of the initiators, and settles disputes among Santeros.

Spiritual power is received through the possession of a person by a powerful demon who gives supernatural knowledge and superhuman strength. This is the same phenomenon found in Haitian voodoo, other forms of black magick, and satanism.

Santeria is also a religion of divination and fortune telling. Cowrie shells are cast down, and the way in which they land is believed to explain the future. The Babalawo can also answer questions through divination at a round wooden board called the "Table of Ifa." He can contact the dead or the demon entities the people call Orishas.

The more one studies the practices of witchcraft and paganism around the world, the more similarities one finds. This is not surprising, since they are all empowered by the same spirit, the fallen angel who in his rage and fury opposes God and everything He does.

WHAT SCRIPTURE SAYS

In the book of Leviticus we are warned, "Do not turn to mediums or seek out spiritists, for you will be defiled by them. I am the LORD your God" (Lev. 19:31). And in Leviticus 20:6 we find the penalty God imposes on those who disobey His directive: "I will set my face against the person who turns to mediums and spiritists to prostitute himself by following them, and I will cut him off from his people."

The temptation to be as God is at the heart of our rebellion and lust for power. No creatures are so obsessed by the will to have power as humans are. We love admiration, self-indulgence, and the pleasures of the flesh, but controlling others is the ultimate ego trip. But no one can serve two masters. It is impossible to walk with God and at the same time walk the left-hand path of the occult.

Are you at a crossroads in your life? Have you flirted with the temptations of illicit knowledge and stolen power? If you have, listen to these words:

> See, I set before you today life and prosperity, death and destruction. For I command you today to love the LORD your God, to walk in his ways, and to keep his commands, decrees and laws; then you will live and increase, and the LORD your God will bless you in the land you are entering to possess.
>
> But if your heart turns away and you are not obedient, and if you are drawn away to bow down to other gods and worship them, I declare to you this day that you will certainly be destroyed.
>
> (Deut. 30:15–18)

Never before has Satan been so bold, so public, so intent on keeping people from Jesus Christ. The serpent of Genesis has grown into the dragon of Revelation. The seduction of supernatural, spiritual power is evident in the increase of occult bookstores, heavy metal and black metal rock music, witchcraft, the New Age, and Satan worship. People are fascinated by the abundance of demonic movies, television shows, and even Saturday morning cartoons that glorify and fantasize the demonic. But the demon realm is not a fantasy; it is not a cartoon world to be toyed and flirted with. Its snares are subtle, but its grasp is fierce; once caught, many never escape its tentacles.

The ironic thing about this seduction is that the power of Satan always leads to self-destruction. In contrast, the power of God, which He freely offers us through His Son, Jesus, invariably builds, strengthens, and beautifies us. Why do so many trade the real for the counterfeit, the truth for a lie, abundant life for despair and destruction?

If you have "played" with the occult in even the mildest form, repent now and ask God to forgive you and set you free from its evil influence. Destroy anything you possess that is occultic in nature. Tell Satan in no uncertain terms that you want nothing further to do with him. Find a group of believing Christians with whom to fellowship and begin to grow in the love of God and the legitimate knowledge and power that is freely granted to all Christians. As the apostle Paul prayed for the early church, so I pray for you:

> I keep asking that the God of our Lord Jesus Christ, the glorious Father, may give you the Spirit of wisdom and revelation, so that you may know him better. I pray also that the eyes of your heart may be enlightened in order that you may know the hope to which he has called you, the riches of his glorious inheritance in the saints, and his incomparably great power for us who believe. . . .
>
> For this reason I kneel before the Father, from whom his whole family in heaven and on earth derives its name. I pray that out of his glorious riches he may strengthen you with power through his Spirit in your inner being, so that

Christ may dwell in your hearts through faith. And I pray that you, being rooted and established in love, may have power, together with all the saints, to grasp how wide and long and high and deep is the love of Christ, and to know this love that surpasses knowledge—that you may be filled to the measure of all the fullness of God.

Now to him who is able to do immeasurably more than all we ask or imagine, according to his power that is at work within us, to him be glory in the church and in Christ Jesus throughout all generations, for ever and ever! Amen.

(Eph. 1:17–19; 3:14–21)

6

SATANISM

The great dragon was hurled down—that
ancient serpent called the devil or Satan,
who leads the whole world astray.

(Rev. 12:9)

DR. JOEL NORRIS and Jerry Allen Potter wrote an article
in which they characterize satanism as "a nightmare come
true, a nationwide epidemic of evil."[1] They report bizarre
and horrifying crimes committed in the name of Satan. In
shocked response to their own discoveries, they wonder
whether it could all be true.

> Is Satanism indeed a hard reality in America, or is it a
> psychiatric metaphor for a society going mad? Perhaps
> both.
> While it is possible that some individuals might be using
> Satanism as a convenient scapegoat for the horrible tortures
> suffered during their childhoods, the sheer number telling
> similar tales argues against this. But could it possibly be this
> bad?[2]

Not only is it as bad as reported, it is worse than we ever

imagined and seems headed toward becoming even more open and destructive. We might be tempted to despair in the face of its horrors if we did not know that the final victory belongs to the Lord Jesus Christ.

Most people in the western world really don't believe in the existence of evil and the spiritual reality of God and Satan. This makes it difficult to confront Satan and satanism in all its varieties. Daily, police discover ritualistic murders of children, adults, and animals, as well as incest, torture, and the worst forms of sexual abuse.

Americans would rather use sociology, psychology, and psychiatry to explain these bizarre behaviors from a human, scientific frame of reference. They simply don't want to face the spiritual reality implied by the evidence. But if we fail to understand satanism and view it as just another cult, albeit a bizarre one, we will be impotent to resist it or save and heal its victims.

Hartgrove Hospital in Chicago opened a psychiatric unit in 1989 for young people who were experimenting with satanism. The treatment modality is traditional psychotherapy and confrontation, similar to the approaches used to treat drug abusers. I commend their recognition that this is a significant and growing problem for young people; yet I am concerned about their refusal to recognize the spiritual implications of the problem. I talked with a staff member about whether there was anyone who could pray with the kids or perform an exorcism if it was needed. The answer was no. Even if a hospital wanted a pastor or priest to perform an exorcism, they would have a difficult time finding one equipped to do it.

WHO IS A SATANIST?

Naturally, most satanists don't make their activities public, but a few flamboyant leaders have emerged. Anton La Vey formed the Church of Satan on April 30, 1966, in San

Francisco. The date was chosen because it is known as Walpurgis Night, a satanic high day like Halloween. La Vey used a carnival atmosphere to lend a "show-biz" flavor to the worship of Satan. He shaved his head and was seen driving a custom-built black hearse. He walked around the streets of San Francisco leading a lion.

La Vey declared himself to be the "black pope of Satanism," but his most lasting impact was his authorship of the *Satanic Bible*. Even though the Church of Satan has received more than its share of publicity, it has never grown very large.

Michael Aquino, formerly a follower of La Vey, formed the Temple of Set in 1975, taking the name from a mythological Egyptian god of death. Aquino is a highly visible spokesperson for satanism and is often seen on television talk shows. His approach is intellectual. He has a Ph.D. in political science and is a lieutenant colonel in the United States Army, with top secret clearance. He practices black magick and is a Nazi sympathizer. The number of followers of the Temple of Set is small, so nationally it would not appear to be a real danger.

How can one evaluate the influences of La Vey and Aquino? I believe they have less power than they think. Yet the real danger of focusing on them is in coming to the conclusion that satanism is not a serious menace in our times. We need to look beneath its show business surface to discover the extent to which its tentacles have reached into our national life. We can perhaps best define the movement by discussing four levels of involvement within it.

THE FIRST LEVEL: EXPERIMENTATION

The entrance to Satan's realm is through the occult. Experimenters or dabblers may begin by reading books on witchcraft and occult practices. Many then progress to using Ouija boards, tarot cards, or the Dungeons and Dragons game. Some visit seances or attempt astral travel. Many young people enter through the door of heavy metal music with satanic or violent lyrics. These experimenters entering the left-hand path are unaware of the danger to their lives.

A Little Experiment

A number of years ago a fourteen-year-old boy called me for an appointment and some days later he and his mother stepped nervously into my office. In the course of the interview, the boy disclosed he had been using drugs and was lonely at school and at home. Consequently he began to read books on witchcraft and to practice spells.

"One day I wanted to see if I could conjure up a demon from the earth, so I made a circle in my back yard," he began. "I started chanting, commanding a demon to appear. It worked! A huge demon appeared in the circle and I was terrified. I didn't know what to do with him. I believe now I have demons in me and I'm really scared."

I explained to him what steps he needed to take to prepare for an exorcism. I wanted him to think about it and be serious when he came for his next appointment. However, he cancelled the appointment, and I didn't hear from him again for another four years. Then he called one morning and asked if I remembered him. He said he had accepted Jesus Christ as Savior and was working through deliverance with his pastor.

"I just wasn't ready to go all the way with Jesus when I met you four years ago," he said sheepishly. It's a good thing the Lord gives us second chances.

Only Once

Not all experimenters in satanism will necessarily be invaded by demons, but sometimes it takes only one contact to be lured into the dark side. An eighteen-year-old girl and her mother came to see me. The unhappy young lady had run away from home at one time, used drugs, and gotten pregnant out of wedlock. According to her mother, previously the girl had been an ideal teenager; the changes occurred abruptly and without warning.

I asked the daughter if she had ever been involved in occult activities. She replied, "Only once," and told about going to a friend's house and playing with a Ouija board.

"What happened?" I asked.

"It went crazy and an evil spirit appeared. I was so frightened! I told my friend I was going home and that I never wanted to see her again. She had told me she was practicing witchcraft, but I didn't believe her until that night!"

"Was your friend angry at you for leaving and dropping her?" I wondered.

"Oh, she was really mad at me."

"Do you think she could have cursed you?" A startled look came over her face.

"I never thought of that, but right afterward I went into a deep depression that lasted a long time, and everything went wrong at home."

I felt there was a strong possibility she had been cursed, and she gave me permission to break the curse. I gently placed my hands on her head, asking for the power of the Holy Spirit. I prayed for the curse of witchcraft to be broken, and commanded the demon assigned to her to leave. Her face changed in appearance as something left her and she was filled with the joy of the Holy Spirit.

THE SECOND LEVEL: INDEPENDENT CULTS

A deeper level of involvement comes with self-styled satanists, or independent cults. Members of these groups meet regularly to perform rituals and devise evil. Members have high levels of commitment and serious addiction to satanic practices. It is not unusual for these self-styled oc-

cultists to turn up in the news. Many serial killers, the
"Night Stalker," Richard Ramirez, for example, are admitted satanists. Ramirez was suspected in some twenty grue-
some murders and two dozen sexual attacks. He was
known to be into drugs and heavy metal music, and he had
a tattoo artist carve a pentagram on his hand. In some
cases, links to satanism have been uncovered in investiga-
tions but were suppressed by police, seeking to avert
"copycat" crimes.

Police departments across the country are finding increasing evidence of satanism at crime scenes, such as symbols of the pentagram, upside-down crosses, the number of
the Antichrist (666), dead animals, circles drawn on the
floor or ground, ritual tools, and the satanic bible.

The national news is chilling. Three teenagers in Mis-
souri bludgeoned a classmate to death in an act of Satan
worship. A popular fifteen-year-old boy in Vermont put a
rifle to his head and committed suicide at Satan's behest.
Four men in Arizona were arrested for desecration of
graves and theft of body parts. At their home, along with
the head of a victim, police found and confiscated satanic
symbols and paraphernalia.

The Son of Sam

David Berkowitz, a killer who came to be known as the
"Son of Sam," terrorized New York, Texas, North Dakota,
and California. Writer Maury Terry researched Berkowitz
for over seven years and disclosed vital evidence about the
murders in his book, *The Ultimate Evil*.[3] Terry discovered
a group of satanists was involved in the killings.

According to Terry, police suppressed a letter found in
Berkowitz' apartment at the time of his arrest. The letter
reveals:

> This warning to all police agencies in the tri-state area.
> For your information, a Satanic cult has been established.

. . . [They] plan to kill at least 100 young women and men . . . as part of a Satanic ritual which involves the shedding of the victims' innocent blood.[4]

Berkowitz also wrote to a minister about his ties with satanism:

At one time I was a member of an occult group. Being sworn to secrecy or death I cannot reveal the name of the group, nor do I wish to. This group contained a mixture of Satanic practices, including the teachings of Aleister Crowley and Eliphas Levi. It was and is totally blood oriented and I am certain you know just what I mean. The coven's doctrines are a blend of ancient Druidism . . . the secret orders of the Golden Dawn, black magick, and a host of other unlawful and obnoxious practices.

To break away completely is impossible because of a pact each new member signs in his own blood. Also each new and carefully screened recruit supplies a picture . . . of all his family, plus their addresses. These items are used, if necessary, as tools for blackmail, coercion, and eventually physical harm should one attempt to betray the group.[5]

Aleister Crowley

In order to understand the evolution of this level of satanism in the United States, we need to discuss one of its early leaders and the influence he has had on the movement.

Aleister Crowley was born in England in 1875. He has been described as the driving force of satanism in England during his lifetime. Today his writings are experiencing a revival among occultists in the United States. Crowley was raised in a very strict Christian sect called the Plymouth Brethren. Even as a young child, he was obsessed with sex. It is said this drive caused his mother to nickname him "The Beast," a reference to an evil world ruler in the book of Revelation.

At age twenty-three Crowley joined the Hermetic Order of the Golden Dawn. This society attempted to draw together all that was best in the ancient magical traditions of Hermeticism and Cabalism, a Hebrew mystical tradition based on numerological interpretations of the Old Testament.

The members of the Golden Dawn believed they had power over demons through their magical incantations. Unfortunately, too many of their leaders were driven by cravings for power. Gerald Yorke, a friend of Crowley's, concluded that the story of the Golden Dawn demonstrates that the occult path of power makes its followers victims of their own creative imaginations and inflated egos.[6]

At twenty-eight, Crowley visited Cairo, Egypt, where he encountered a demon entity called Aiwuz while in a trance. The demon dictated what became *The Book of the Law*. The main thrust of the book is "do what you will," or be a law unto yourself.

By 1912 Crowley had discovered another magical organization, The Order of the Temple of the Orient. It was there that he came upon Tantra Yoga and the power of sexual energy to drive men and women toward higher consciousness. His belief in Tantra Yoga and the introduction of sex magic and sexual rights into satanism remained a driving force throughout Crowley's life, and sowed the tragic seeds that victims and therapists are reaping today.[7]

Aleister Crowley became the most powerful satanist in England, reigning as undisputed head of the movement from 1920 to 1930. His creed was, "Be strong, O man! Lust! Enjoy all the things of sense. Fear not that any god shall deny thee for this!" He became addicted to heroin and cocaine and was accused of being a homosexual, a child molester, and a sexual deviant. It was also said that he sacrificed infants in occult rituals. He died a poverty-stricken drug addict in 1947.[8] Clearly, he was a demon possessed and driven man.

Tantra Yoga

The practices learned by Crowley from Tantra Yoga introduced the horrifying sexual rituals that have become an integral part of satanism today. When you investigate the story of the Hindu god Shiva and goddess Kali, you gain some understanding of their influence on American satanic practices.

Kali is a goddess with a cruel side, who is known as both the creator, or life giver, and the destroyer. She is depicted smeared with blood, wearing a garland made of human heads, and chewing flesh.[9] Dressed in scarlet, she demands blood sacrifices, just as Satan does.

Shiva, Kali's soul-twin and husband, is similarly bloodthirsty. They become one through sexual union; thus in calling on Shiva, Hindus also call on Kali. New Agers who practice Tantra Yoga maintain that through sexual union they link up with the energy of the universe.[10]

Salem Kirban, in his book *Satan's Angels Exposed,* states his belief that Tantra Yoga is one of the most satanic cults of the East. Much of Western cult practices have been influenced by the Tantrists of India. From them have come the ceremonial magic of candles, incense, bells, magic wands and circles, spells, body postures, occult gestures, symbolic designs, and words of power. Tantrism dwells on sexual excess, advocating complete sexual freedom which is thought of as a trait of divinity.[11]

This second level of satanism, including the many independent cults and covens, is the one most Americans are likely to hear about. It is becoming alarmingly widespread, and is particularly dangerous in its attractiveness to youth.

THE THIRD LEVEL: SATANISM THROUGH GENERATIONS

There are some families in which satanism has been practiced for generations, its secrets being passed from parent to child and from one generation to the next. These groups, who reach back into the past, tend to be much more secretive about their practices and their members. There are no written records of membership; contracts with Satan are signed by members in their own blood and then burned by high priests or priestesses. One such group is called the Brotherhood. It draws membership from all walks of life. Among the ranks are physicians, psychologists, professors, successful businessmen, morticians, judges, policemen, government officials, members of the entertainment industry, and even ministers. Most of them attend local Christian churches where they are often leaders. They are praised as outstanding citizens because of their civic activities. A former member of the Brotherhood told me his grandmother was a high priestess of Satan who, when she died, was given a huge civic funeral. Her minister and the leaders of the community praised her for all she had done as a civic leader and patroness of the community.

Groups such as the Brotherhood regularly practice human as well as animal sacrifice. Incest is regarded as a normal, expected activity, as is eating human flesh and drinking blood. They are careful that no trace can ever be found. They often have a portable crematorium to use in disposing of the bodies of their victims. They thoroughly cleanse their meeting places, leaving no clue of their heinous activities. Because of their care, law enforcement officials have difficulty investigating them, and they rarely appear in the news media.

Such groups would never announce in the media that they are starting a satanist church, for secrecy is a top priority, and severe punishment is given to those who break it. The Brotherhood has a very effective network across the country. They are able to control and keep in touch with members, especially those who wish to leave. But, praise God, people *are* leaving the Brotherhood and being set free by Jesus Christ.

THE FOURTH LEVEL: THE ILLUMINATI

The deepest level of satanism belongs to the Illuminati, which means "Holders of the Light." These people profess to have special intellectual or spiritual enlightenment. Lucifer is called "Light Bearer," or "enlightened one," hence the name Illuminati is derived from him.

The Order of the Illuminati was founded by Dr. Adam Weishaupt on May 1, 1776. A professor of canon law at the University of Ingolostadt in Bavaria, Weishaupt was a Jew who converted to Roman Catholicism. He became a Jesuit priest only to break with the church later and form his own secret society. The organization he created held the following goals:[12]

- Abolition of all ordered government
- Abolition of private property
- Abolition of inheritances
- Abolition of patriotism
- Abolition of all religions
- Abolition of the family
- Creation of a world government

Weishaupt led the formation of an alliance between the Illuminati and Freemasonry in 1782. Eventually the Bavarian government acted to ban both the Illuminati and the Freemasons in 1785. Dr. Weishaupt was forced to leave the country. Four leading members of the Illuminati testified before a Bavarian Court of Inquiry exposing the satanic notions of the organization and its goals. Illuminati oppose both Christianity and atheism, and seek to enthrone Satan, whom they call Lucifer, as god.[13] There is still very little public knowledge about this high level international organization. It is known, however, that Illuminati are very powerful and dangerous satanists who practice human sacrifice. They are believed to have connections to the Brotherhood; beyond that, their activities are shrouded in mystery.

SATAN WORSHIP

Satan worship began in heaven when Satan rebelled against God and recruited other angels to follow and submit to him. Cast out of heaven, he invaded earth to seek worshipers and power. He came to "steal, kill and destroy" (John 10:10), and his followers are actively fulfilling this mandate. In the next pages, the details of his worship may shock you. They are not fantasy, however, but have been testified to over and over again by those who have escaped alive from Satan's wrath.

THE BLACK MASS

The Black Mass was developed in the Middle Ages for the purpose of mocking God and worshiping Satan. Satanic days of celebration come during the special holy days of Christendom: Thanksgiving, Christmas, and Easter. Other special days have also been added, including Halloween, Walpurgis Night, and the first days of spring, summer, fall, and winter.

The Setting

The Black Mass is often held in an abandoned church building as an added form of blasphemy. If no church is available, a home or other abandoned building or a secluded outdoor setting is used.

If the ritual is held in a home, the walls are draped in black fabric. The only light is from candles and the glow of a black kettle on the floor, usually heated by an electric hot plate.

A large five-pointed star, the pentagram, is drawn on the floor with a circle around it. The circle must be completely closed so that when a demon is summoned, the priest will be protected. A black candle is placed in each corner of the pentagram and a much larger candle in the center. The kettle is filled with holy water from a Catholic church. Usually the blood of an animal, urine, or other potions are mixed with the water.

An altar, usually made of stone, is draped in red velvet. The Christian cross is hung upside down. There is often a goat head of Mendes over the altar. Anything that blasphemes God is used. Sacramental wafers, usually stolen from a church, are scattered on the floor to be trampled or urinated upon by the participants. Praise and worship are given to Satan. Censers for burning incense are used, but drugs are placed in them instead of incense. The Christian liturgy is recited backward and revised to worship Satan, whose name is chanted backward as Natas.

A client who was raised in satanism recited for me this version of the Lord's Prayer:

> Our father who art the ruler of the underworld.
> Hallowed be thy name.
> Thy kingdom come,
> Thy will be done on earth as it is in your kingdom.
> Give us this day our daily flesh,
> And forgive us our transgressions.
> Lead us into each and every temptation,
> And bestow upon us increasing amounts of your
> Evil, mighty power.
> For thine is the glory forever. Amen.
> Hail Almighty Father Satan!

The Worshipers

Worshipers wear black robes with hoods trimmed in red and bearing satanic emblems. The robes are open in front, and the participants are otherwise naked with their genitals exposed. The celebrants begin to hum, chant, and pray to Satan. As the high priest approaches, the chanting takes on the form, "All hail to the father Satan. All hail to the father Satan! All hail to Natas!"

The high priest takes a sword from the altar and points it to the north, south, east, and west. He begins to ask Satan for a demon to appear in the pentagram to do the priest's bidding. Demons are compelled to obey his commands. If someone is cursed, the demon is sent to enact the curse. Other demons are called to give the coven members more power.

Ceremonial Horrors

Cult members believe that cannibalism and drinking blood give them power and that babies' bodies and blood give the most power. Because of these beliefs, ritual ceremonies include brutalizing victims with practices that are beyond human depravity and so bizarre they could only be demonically inspired.

I have worked with several people who were raised in satanic families or were satanist themselves and later renounced satanism and its horrors. Their stories are so horrible the reaction of the average person is that these things couldn't possibly be true. But they are. No depravity is too much for Satan. He and his demons direct their followers to brutalize their victims, drink their blood, eat portions of their bodies, torture them mercilessly, and ultimately kill them. It is truly a miracle of God that some survive.

Drinking Blood

Drinking blood, whether human or animal, is a basic part of Satan worship. I have come to understand what God meant in Leviticus 17:10–11. "Any Israelite or any alien living among them who eats any blood—I will set my face against that person who eats blood and will cut him off from his people. For the life of a creature is in the blood, and I have given it to you to make atonement for yourselves on the altar; it is the blood that makes atonement for one's life."

The November 1989 issue of *Psychology Today* features the article, "The Vampire Craze in the Computer Age." The article warns of an impending slew of vampire entertainment. Experts are quoted describing "people who participate in a secret vampire world that sometimes overlaps with sadomasochistic cults across the country. They find peace, strength, and satisfaction in drinking blood they extract in various ways—with needles, sometimes through a bite, sometimes through whippings and beatings."[14] Satan is gradually getting our society to accept deviant, bizarre, and heartless behavior as normal. From excessive and continual violence in films to the acceptance of abortion on a massive scale, Satan is delighted with anything that will "steal, kill, and destroy."

Finding Children for Sacrifice

The main way to obtain infant victims is to produce them. In satanic cults there are women called breeders whose sole purpose is to produce babies for sacrifice. I have known personally and worked with women who have undergone numerous abortions to produce sacrificial babies. It is considered a high honor for satanist parents to give Satan the sacrifice of their own child on a high holiday.

I once ministered to a woman raised by satanist parents. While she was still in the womb, they dedicated her to Satan. Later they baptized her in the blood of an animal. As a teen, she was presented to be a bride of Satan. She participated in rituals, including human sacrifice. She was prepared to accept that when she reached the age of twenty-five it would be her great honor to be sacrificed on the altar. But when the time drew near, she fled for her life and lived on the run for many years. Each year on the anniversary date of her intended "wedding," she had to fight the urge to commit suicide. Only when she came for exorcism and inner healing was she set free of the compulsion to kill herself for her "betrayal" of Satan.

SATANIC PROFIT MOTIVE

We should not overlook the tremendous amount of money that can be made by those who follow Satan. Perhaps this profit motive is part of what energizes the movement; it certainly must be used to finance it.

Satanists use children not only for sacrifice, but for child prostitution as well. Many pedophiles pay handsomely to satisfy their cravings. Children are filmed for the lucrative trade in child pornography. These films can also serve as material for blackmail if a victim later wants to leave or expose a cult. Police investigators are reviewing the cases of all the children reported missing a few years ago in Atlanta, looking for links to satanism.

Adult women are also used for prostitution and pornography by satanist cults or covens. First hooked on drugs, they will then do anything to get more. Covens have been linked to drug dealing networks with their massive profits and to laundering money.

Finally, they have learned to make murder profitable. Maury Terry, in his book *The Ultimate Evil,* states he believes the evidence he uncovered points to a network of satanic cults across the country specializing in murder. Often bloody torture and murder of adults or children are filmed while in progress and then sold as a unique genre of movies called "snuff" films. The existence of snuff films has been thoroughly documented in the press.

APPEAL TO YOUTH

One of the most frightening things about Satanism today is that so many of our nation's youth are attracted to satanic cults. Gangs such as the Stoners, Neo-Nazi groups, and

Skinheads are heavily into the occult, satanism, drugs, black magick, reincarnation, and astral travel. They have been known to drink blood and eat the hearts of their victims. In juvenile hall settings, Stoners have been observed to be fascinated with blood, urine, and feces, often drinking, eating, and smearing them.[15]

A 1986 report by the Task Force on Youth Gang Violence of the California Council on Criminal Justice revealed some startling and troubling facts:

> Heavy metal, punk rockers, and Satanic groups have emerged as new gang phenomena [and] greatly differ from the more traditional street gangs. Most of their activities are secretive and, therefore, hard to identify. The characteristics of these gangs are: members are predominantly white and of a middle class socioeconomic status; they listen to heavy metal rock music; nothing traditionally held sacred is recognized; their behavior is violent—they enjoy shock value; they have little parental authority and believe in anarchy; and their goal is to destroy, not protect. These groups' activities include drawing graffiti, using illegal drugs, abusing children, and assaulting parents. Grave robbing and desecration of animal and human remains are some of the more bizarre activities associated with these groups.[16]

I have worked with troubled teens for more than twenty years, and I find what is happening today very frightening. I believe the bizarre and violent acts we are observing today are impossible to explain with normal psychological theories alone. There must be satanic power and purpose behind them.

Heavy metal music has a strong influence on these young people. On a subconscious level, they cannot help but react to lyrics like those that call Satan "father" and speak of becoming strong demon warriors and satanic royalty, as well as slaves to hell and blasphemy.

Ronnie James Dio, on his album *Dream Evil,* depicts a child asleep in bed. Satan peers through a window above her, flashing his two-fingered salute. Evil creatures and slithering snakes crawl from beneath the bed. The group Iron Maiden has a favorite subject: sorcery and savagery. Their first hit was the album *Number of the Beast,* featuring a song dedicated to the Antichrist. The cover of *Seventh Son of a Seventh Son* depicts a ghoulish mascot symbolizing death holding a ripped-out heart.[17]

At high schools and colleges there are groups who offer the young people free drugs and sex, and after these parties they search out those who could become more deeply involved in satanism.

According to the Cult Awareness Network, the child most likely to be drawn in is the teenager seeking excitement. He or she is usually bored and underachieving. A bright, often talented and gifted, young person whose sense of self-worth is low is especially vulnerable.[18]

In later chapters we will explore the symptoms that parents should be aware of and strategies for helping teens who have become ensnared by satanism.

PRINCIPLES OF SATANISM

Anton La Vey, founder of the First Church of Satan, articulated some of the foundational principles of satanism. These are the motives and theological beliefs that guide satanists. La Vey's statements make clear that satanism is the utter opposite of Christianity:

- Satan represents indulgence instead of abstinence.
- Satan represents vital existence instead of spiritual dreams.
- Satan represents undefiled wisdom instead of hypocritical self-deceit.

- Satan represents kindness to those who deserve it instead of love wasted on ingrates.
- Satan represents vengeance instead of turning the other cheek.
- Satan represents man as just another animal, sometimes better [but] more often worse than those who walk on all fours. . . . [Man] has become the most vicious animal of all.
- Satan represents all of the so-called sins [because] they lead to physical, mental, or emotional gratification.[19]

In order for us to fully understand the extent and danger of satanism in our country today, we must look more closely into the phenomenon that is horrifying pastors, therapists, and clinicians across the country: Satanic ritual abuse.

7

✳

SATANIC RITUAL ABUSE

You are of your father the devil, and the
desires of your father you want to do. He
was a murderer from the beginning.

(John 8:44)

IN AUGUST 1983, Judy Johnson of Manhattan Beach,
California, noticed a rectal irritation and blood in her two-
and-a-half-year-old son's diaper. A physician confirmed her
worst fears: the child had been sodomized. When asked
who did it, the little boy simply said, "Mister Ray." Judy
Johnson knew that to be Raymond Buckey, a teacher at the
McMartin Preschool where she had enrolled her son three
months earlier.

A short time later Buckey was arrested based on Judy
Johnson's complaint, and police began an investigation.
Three hundred eighty-nine former students of the school
were interviewed, and all reported sexual abuse. The preschool was closed, and seven people were charged in 108
counts of sexual molestation. Eighty percent of the students bore physical evidence to substantiate their testimo-
nies, including scar tissue of the vagina and anus, rectal
bleeding, and painful bowel movements.

At the preliminary hearing in Los Angeles, a ten-year-old boy testified that he and other children were forced to dig up bodies at a local cemetery and watch while some of their teachers hacked at the corpses with knives. Several other children described being compelled to drink rabbit blood during a satanic ceremony held near the school. Adults wearing black robes moaned and chanted in whirling circles around the children. A rabbit was killed in front of them as a graphic demonstration of what would happen to their parents if they told anyone what they had witnessed.

In January 1986 charges against five of the teachers were dropped. Only Raymond Buckey and his mother, Peggy McMartin Buckey, went to trial. The trial lasted thirty-three months and cost $15,000,000, making it the longest and costliest trial in United States history. On January 18, 1990, after nine weeks of deliberation, an exhausted and emotionally drained Los Angeles jury acquitted Buckey and McMartin on fifty-two counts and declared it was deadlocked on thirteen others.[1]

> For many, the case stood as a sad indictment of a legal system that had neither the experience nor the sensitivity to deal with profoundly disturbing sex abuse charges on so great a scale. After 63,000 pages of testimony, 917 exhibits, and 24 witnesses, there was only one thing the opposing sides seemed to agree on: police and prosecutors had made serious errors preparing and presenting the case. What never emerged, according to some observers, was the truth.[2]

UNWILLING TO KNOW

The McMartin horror story is not an isolated one. The media have reported similar ritualistic sex crimes at the West Point Preschool in Fort Bragg, North Carolina, and the Army Presidio Day Care Center in San Francisco. Across the country, children are disclosing acts of ritualistic sexual abuse, sacrifice of animals and humans, torture, and fear.

Americans are having a hard time coming to grips with the extent of child sexual abuse. When satanic black masses, human sacrifices, and ritualistic horror stories are added, the result is overwhelming and stretches the credulity of the public. It is essential that parents, teachers, law enforcement officials, and clinical professionals take children seriously when they report abuse, even if their stories seem bizarre.

Listen to Your Preschooler

Finding a safe preschool environment for your child can be a tremendous challenge. Dr. Catherine Gould, a clinical psychologist who works with sexually and ritualistically abused children, cautions parents about lightly assuming that a preschool is safe. The so-called "open" preschools, for instance, invite parents to drop in at any time and walk directly into the classroom. However, a "watch" person can alert perpetrators that a parent is arriving, and the child can be produced quickly, avoiding parental suspicion of wrongdoing.

Gould says that personnel at offending schools usually do not seem "strange." In fact, they may be very solicitous concerning the children's progress. But the expense, prestige, and religious or educational affiliation of a preschool seem to provide no assurance that the school is safe. Gould has noted that satanic ritual abusers tend to infiltrate preschools in clusters by geographic area.[3]

In choosing a preschool, parents should take the obvious precautions of looking for licensure, inspecting the premises, and discussing the program with administrators and teachers. However, they should also talk extensively with other parents whose children attended the school in the past, and they need to make sure these children attended for periods long enough for their parents to make a realistic evaluation of the school.

Finally, if you have enrolled your children in a pre-school, *talk with them* often about their school experiences. If you suspect that your child is being abused, remove him or her from the school immediately. Confronting the school's administrators with the child's allegations of abuse will only produce denials. Instead, you should contact someone in the police department who is experienced in this type of investigation. The most important thing you should do is *believe your child!*

RITUAL ABUSE DEFINED

Ritual abuse is any kind of repeated abusive process involving rituals. It can occur, for instance, between a husband and wife. The "ritual" might be that every Friday night the husband gets drunk and beats the wife. It is a ritual because it is predictable and repeated, and it develops characteristic patterns. Repeated painful abuse results in long-term emotional damage requiring a difficult and lengthy healing process.

Satanic ritual abuse is repeated abuse associated with the worship of Satan. When ritual abuse is coupled with satanism, it takes on another dimension that complicates the healing process. Therapists have to deal not only with the emotional devastation of the abuse, but also with the spiritual repercussions. Not the least of these are the demonic entities that attach themselves to abuse victims—speaking through them, controlling their thoughts and actions, and creating utter confusion in their minds.

Satanic ritual abuse is the most difficult form of abuse a therapist encounters and, unfortunately, few counselors are equipped to deal with it. Many disbelieve in the spiritual nature of the battle and refuse to acknowledge the demons that may be interfering with the healing process.

One secular psychologist says, "Therapists must assume the position that abusers were terribly confused and sick, as opposed to instruments of the devil. Such a therapeutic position is an essential ingredient in the necessary demystification process that should occur in the treatment surrounding the abuse."[4]

The secular mode of psychotherapy does not recognize the supernatural, Satan, or God. Children who have seen demonic spirits and experienced their hideous power quickly understand that the therapist will not believe them. Quickly they learn to say, "I won't tell the doctor the things he won't believe," and the candle of hope for them grows even dimmer.

My personal belief is that every adult survivor of satanic ritual abuse needs an exorcism of demonic spirits. Otherwise his healing will not be complete.

The Extent of Abuse

Dr. Dave Griffin reported a 1990 survey intended to document awareness and incidences of ritual crime activity. He found stunning results.

- Ten years ago, only 2 percent of police departments were receiving inquiries about ritual crimes.
- Ten years ago, only 8 percent of mental health professionals had ever heard about ritual crimes and abuse, and educators were completely unaware of the problem.
- Between 1987 and 1988, 87 percent of the therapists and 78 percent of the law enforcement officials surveyed had cases involving ritual crimes.
- 100 percent of the schools responding had some form of occult activity.[5]

Many satanic ritual abuse victims experience a kind of amnesia, a mental process of repressing memories in order to cope with their horror and attempt to live normal lives. But now the amnesia seems to be lifting. Is it because the awareness of abuse has become more public? This may be a factor, but I also believe that God is working to expose Satan and arouse the church to action. The tragic stories these survivors tell of unspeakable horror, torture, and murder are forcing us to see the reality of Satan in our world. The stories shock and sicken, but perhaps we need "shock therapy" to awaken us and make us aware of the destruction that is taking place all around us.

The greatest fear of the survivors of this hell is that they won't be believed. A survivor of satanic ritual abuse has given me permission to quote her on this subject.

> Survivors' first need is to feel safe. They must feel safe in the present to face the inside terror of their past. In order to feel safe, they must be believed, accepted, and loved. You must listen with your heart as well as your head, your eyes and ears. They will know if you are trying to fake it. They will know if you haven't dealt with your issues on the subject. They will care about you. You must also care genuinely about them. They are fragile and yet as hard and tough as diamonds. Remember, they have already done more by themselves, often as tiny babies and preschoolers, than most adults are capable of doing.

Mary's Story

It wasn't until 1986 that I encountered an adult survivor of satanic ritual abuse. Her name was Mary. She had just turned fifty when she came to me for inner healing and exorcism. For years she'd sought healing, but all the counselors and pastors she talked to either didn't believe her or failed to understand that she needed exorcism as well as healing.

Mary was raised by seemingly devout Christian parents who were active in their church and upstanding citizens in their community. But the mother and father and a grandfather, who lived with them, were all satanists. Mary was a disappointment to her parents because she wasn't a boy. Her grandfather and father began to sexually abuse her when she was a young child.

One haunting memory of her childhood was a trip to her grandfather's bedroom where she was tied to his bed, sexually assaulted, and physically tormented. A physician, who was also a high priest in the satanic cult, participated. Mary remembers that they put a rag over her mouth, containing just enough ether to keep her helpless. They shaved her head, drew blood, cut her skin with surgical knives, and marked her for Satan.

Mary also remembers being taken to a warehouse for a black mass. There were animals in cages, and chains attached to the walls where victims were bound and then sodomized and beaten. Mary was stretched across the altar and tortured and raped. Live animals were sacrificed on top of her. Somehow she survived that night. During her therapy, countless other horrible memories surfaced and, before she was healed, many demonic spirits were cast out from her.

Missing Foundations

The significant thing I have learned in working with adult survivors is that these people lack the normal emotional and psychological foundations of childhood development. They have no frame of reference with which to understand words like *love, trust, hope,* or *joy.* They have no basis for knowing what is normal and what is sick or demonic. Because they are programmed all their lives to be victims, they easily assume the victim role in marriage, at work, with friends, and/or with their families. Healing includes not only dealing with their personal rage, helplessness, and fear, but the remapping of all their relational structures. As I discovered with Lynn, even their relationship with God has to be reformed.

Lynn's Story

Lynn's parents were alcoholics, abusers, and satanists. During the months after she came to me, Lynn tried to help me understand that, because of the abuse she suffered as a child, she had no basis for comparing a normal, good life with a life that had always been a living hell. She described the way her parents perverted all normal ideas of God and, therefore, in her young child's mind, she believed God was a cruel tormentor.

> How could I believe in love, when I had never known love from my parents? How could I believe in a God of love, when my father, who was supposed to love me, tortured and raped me? A God of love? Everything I had learned of God from my parents and the other Satanists was a lie, a perversion of God.
>
> Am I angry at my parents? Anger isn't strong enough to express the murderous rage I feel inside. Am I angry with God? Why shouldn't I be angry with God? Who *is* God, and where was God when this endless nightmare of torture and pain was happening to me? Am I filled with blasphemous emotions and thoughts toward God? You better believe it!

I admit I had a difficult time with Lynn's blasphemy. I needed to separate it into her emotional reactions to satanic programming aimed at contaminating her belief in a loving God and the work of the demonic spirits of rage and blasphemy. Which part was rage projected toward her father resulting from his abuse of her and then transferred to the Heavenly Father, and which part was demonic activity? At times I did not handle Lynn well.

I pushed her to confess her sin of blasphemy when she

wasn't able to hear me or accept what I asked her to do. I didn't understand the depths of the contamination and confusion satanists will create to keep a person from ever wanting to seek God or to believe in His loving acceptance of sinners and healing through Jesus Christ.

MINDS UNDER CONTROL

The lengths to which satanists go to control the spiritual minds of children is incredible. First, they create confusion about what is good and what is evil, for to a satanist, there is no real evil and no sin. Each person can do as he or she pleases so long as it is pleasing to Satan, whom Jesus called the "father of lies." And the satanists want to prevent abused children from telling anyone what is happening to them. Fear, confusion, hypnosis, electric shock, and mind-altering drugs are only a few of their favored methods.

Lynn revealed some of the messages she received from her parents and other satanists at their rituals:

> You are a little bitch that deserves to die. I hate you and God hates you and Satan owns you, body and soul. You will live a satanist and die a satanist. For you there is no hope. I want you to die. God wants you to die. Everyone wants you to die. Therefore, you will surely die the painful death that you deserve so much.

"They made me sign in my own blood some paper saying I would never tell anyone about any of this," she said, "and if I did, they would kill me. They cut my finger and used my own blood to fill up the pen."

As an adult survivor, Lynn can't stand to sign documents because just being asked to sign anything brings back the old fear. She remembers they promised to get her and kill her by skinning her alive the way they did the baby Jesus. This memory is very vivid. Lynn was made to watch a baby being skinned alive, and the satanists told her the baby was Jesus.

Perhaps the most horrifying memory concerns her sister's death. Lynn saw her sister taken to Satan's altar. She saw her sister look at her with such terror and pleading in her eyes for Lynn to do something to save her. But Lynn was a little girl herself and helpless. She watched her sister be tortured and killed on the altar because she had talked. "She told someone what they were doing, and they killed her for it. They mean it when they say don't tell anyone."

Redefining Truth

A recurring theme in the process of confusing and controlling child victims is the redefining of Christian concepts and symbols. "Lord" and "Father" are used to refer to Satan instead of God. Crucifixes are used as instruments of torture, and the knife used to slaughter victims is called "the sword of the spirit."

Lynn told me of two men in the coven who impersonated God and Jesus. Over and over the children were told, "Obey your father. You must submit to the Lord. You must surrender." To what should they surrender? Sexual rape, drinking a cup of blood, or plunging a knife into the heart of an infant and then eating part of the heart. Young girls are told, "You are chosen of the Lord God," referring, of course, to Satan. "It is an honor to be chosen to submit to this specialist of obedience. The priest will bless you for your submission." Ultimately, they discover that being "special" means they will be sacrificed at a satanic festival.

Consider the emotional confusion and fear the survivors of these practices will later experience if they become Christians. Being told they are "special" to God can incite fear rather than pleasure. A communion service with the words, "Take and eat; this is the body of Christ," and "Take and drink; this is the blood of Christ," can recall tormenting memories for a former victim of blood rituals.

Destroying Trust

Many of the ritually abused tell stories of being put in a coffin with a corpse and a hose to breathe through, and then buried alive. They were told to pray to God or Jesus to save them from the grave. After a period of time, the casket was opened and the child was asked, "Did God or Jesus rescue you from the grave?"

The child answered, "No."

"Did your parents rescue you from the grave?"

"No," the child replied.

Then the high priest would lift the child out of the coffin and say, "Did Satan rescue you from the grave?"

"Yes," the child would meekly reply.

Another common message repeated over and over is, "Your parents don't love you. You are evil. God hates you. Satan is your only hope. Satan owns you, body and soul." The repeated message is that you can never leave satanism. This is graphically reinforced at gatherings where a member of the coven is sacrificed because he or she was discovered attempting to leave the cult.

The purpose of sexually abusing children is not for sexual pleasure but to dominate and terrorize the child and to destroy self-esteem. Trust—in yourself or anyone else—can never be built on the foundations of terror and pain, and without trust, even the conduct of everyday life becomes difficult and painful.

Invading the Mind

The techniques used to control a child's mind are incredible and effective. Satan wants the child to grow up to be an adult who is completely turned away from Christianity and moral values.

Hypnosis and mind-altering drugs are used to open the subconscious mind to programming. Hymns and chants to Satan are repeated continually in a trance-like state. "Satan is Lord; Satan is all-powerful," repeated over and over hundreds of times will, of course, infect the unconscious mind and will.

Another technique is to plant "trigger" words in the subconscious mind that can later cause a person to react in a predictable way. If a person has left a satanic group, an activated trigger could cause him or her to want to return or prompt suicide.

"I frankly am afraid to be around in ten years when these kids are adolescents," says psychologist Catherine Gould. "Satanists are highly experienced in areas of terrorism, mind control, brainwashing, and reinforcement, apparently to gain total control of the child's soul. Their strategy is definitely geared toward manipulating and indoctrinating the coming generation, instilling hatred, destruction, and chaos as the norm."

Dr. Gould continues, "The children have been abused in a way that is meant to make them sadistic. It is meant to make them murderers. It is meant to make them hateful, hurtful individuals."[6]

Breaking the Will

The breaking of a child's free will is necessary so that he or she will do the bidding and accept the beliefs of satanism. Fear, torture, electric shock, deprivation of food and sleep, and dizziness induced by spinning lights are all methods employed to break a child's will. When the child finally crumbles under the torture, she is told she can have power over other people if she surrenders to Satan. This "training period" often goes on for years.

Donna's Story

Donna, whose stepfather was a high priest of Satan, lived through a "training period" one summer when she was eight years old. The memory of that time is best told in her own words.

I was locked in the basement. One of the women satanists was there to teach me everything I needed to know. She was very pretty with pale skin and long, dark hair. Her fingernails were long and polished and she dressed quite smartly. As first I liked her and thought she was nice, but that changed, ever so quickly. She was cruel and vicious, one of the most cold and evil people I have ever met.

Rather than allowing me to come up out of the basement for my lessons, she came down and sat on a step. I was naked and the basement was dark, cold, and damp. It had a dirt floor. I knew there were spiders and other insects all over. There were also rats. I was terrified of the dark, and when she would leave me alone there, I would sit crouched on one step, fearing to move even a little bit, afraid that something in that dark would "get" me. I got bites all over my body. Some were from insects and spiders; others were from rodents.

The first several days I was there, she brought me food and water. Then she withheld both until I thought I would die of hunger and thirst. When she brought me food again, it had living, crawling bugs in it. Even though I was only eight years old and had no understanding of what she wanted from me, I was desperate, willing to do almost anything she asked so that I could get out of that horrible basement.

I had to unlearn everything I had been taught in Sunday school. Everything she taught me was the exact opposite of what I'd been told was "the truth." She said that Satan, not God, was all powerful and all knowing. She called him by many different names—Lucifer, Prince of Darkness, Ruler of the Underworld, Beelzebub, and others. She made me say that I renounced God, Jesus, and the Holy Spirit. I did not know what the word *renounce* meant, but I had a bad feeling about it, so I refused to say it until she made things so miserable for me that I hoped God would understand that I didn't really mean it, whatever it was.

By the time they finally released me from my prison in the basement, several weeks had gone by. I had not bathed or showered in all that time, nor had I combed my hair or brushed my teeth. I looked like a little animal coming out of hibernation. The sun hurt my eyes and it was some time before I could force them open enough to see. The sun felt wonderfully warm on my bare body as they pushed me toward that shiny black car.

August 1 is a special day for satanists and it was for this special day that I was being groomed. As the ritual began, they laid me naked on a cold altar and painted half of my body with green stuff and the other half with blood. Then they began the ritual they call "pointing." They threw me up in the air and then caught me, each time pointing me in a different direction. They did this over and over, pointing me to the east, west, north, and south. They were really rough with me, catching me and grabbing me anywhere on my body.

Next they sacrificed a baby, and they made me slice her open and cut out her heart, which they passed around and ate.

I had to recite all my newly learned knowledge. As I did it, I prayed silently to God that He would understand I didn't mean it. I was doing it only to protect my life, even though by that time I was beginning to doubt it was worth it. I'd begun to develop a death wish—not suicide, but a wish I'd just go to sleep and never wake up or that they would beat me so badly, I'd die. I was eight years old and I felt my life wasn't worth living.

Donna's story illustrates the kind of "training sessions" satanists use to conquer the wills of children. Her tale is not an unusual one; therapists and pastors across the country are hearing similar accounts from children and adults whose very sanity is threatened by the tormented memories and self-destructive programming that was forced on them.

The Ultimate Programming: Murder

A woman with tear-stained face sits in my office, trembling and crying uncontrollably. A memory has surfaced:

She stands before an altar and plunges a knife into a victim. As a powerful, murderous demon takes control, she leaps on the victim in a wild frenzy. Screaming, "Kill, kill, kill—bleed, bleed, bleed!" she proceeds to dismember the body.

Such memories are almost unbearable. The fact that a survivor has participated in taking another person's life leaves him or her with overwhelming guilt and self-hatred. One woman told me her murderous rage became so great she turned on her fellow satanists while they were intoxicated by drugs and began slashing them. Another woman described giving birth to her first child at age twelve, and then killing the infant in a satanic sacrifice.

Victims who have been so terrorized that they will even commit murder are left emotionally devastated. They are filled with a deep, overpowering emotional hopelessness and often are suicidal. Sometimes the feelings of these re-lived horrors are so overpowering that my words have little effect on the person's healing. Only the Holy Spirit can mend a life so shattered.

A TORMENTED WORLD

We have seen a glimpse of the world of the ritual abuse survivor. As we look at these cases, the strategies and methods of Satan begin to emerge:

- Exploit and degrade children whenever possible. Look for victims in nurseries, schools, neighborhoods, and even churches where parents are not vigilant.
- Inhibit normal development by undermining healthy self-esteem and undermine the foundations of growth and stability in childhood.
- Redefine truth to create a maximum amount of confusion, especially about Christian doctrine.
- Destroy trust in family, friends, teachers, and pastors, and especially in God or Christ.

- Invade the mind using hypnosis, trance, drugs, shock, and repetitive programming to indoctrinate with satanic ideas and values.
- Break the will with deprivation, torture, rape, beatings, degradation, and electric shock mixed with praise for submission and promises of power.
- Induce rage and instill deviance, hatred, sadism, destructive and chaotic behavior, and murder.
- Make a profit on all this through prostitution and child and adult pornography.

The task God has set before the church demands that we walk in the footsteps of Jesus and "destroy the works of the devil" (1 John 3:8).

The church must obtain knowledge from the truth of God's Word and be willing to get involved. Secular psychology can go only so far in helping victims like Donna and Lynn. New life in Jesus Christ and the power of the Holy Spirit are the only sources of ultimate peace, freedom, and healing.

PART THREE

Exorcism

For this purpose the Son of God was
manifested, that He might destroy the
works of the devil.

(1 John 3:8)

8

THE ABCS OF POSSESSION

Your adversary the devil walks about like
a roaring lion, seeking whom he may
devour.

(1 Peter 5:8)

HOW DOES A person become possessed? What are the
conditions under which demonic personalities can gain access to human beings to indwell and torment them?

Some traditions hold that possession is a very rare phenomenon in modern times. However, an unusual article appearing in *The Arizona Republic* on March 6, 1990,
indicates there are some who acknowledge demonic possession is a reality and that exorcism is a necessity. Entitled
"Exorcism Conducted in New York, Church Says," the article refers to Cardinal John O'Connor's announcement that
two apparently successful exorcisms, approved by the
vicar general of the Roman Catholic Church's New York
archdiocese were conducted in the New York area during
the previous several months. The cardinal disclosed this information in a sermon and then later to reporters.

O'Connor said what can appear to be demonic possession often has psychological or medical causes, which must be ruled out before possession can be suspected. He also indicated that while demonic possession seems rare, he was alarmed by what he called "satanic rituals in which young people 'engage in disgraceful' practices, sometimes in cemeteries."[1]

Although O'Connor admitted the church is slow to use exorcism, the Rev. Simon Harak, theology professor at Connecticut's Fairfield University, said that "exorcism, which existed before the time of Christ, may gain prevalence in times or places of satanic worship."[2] Yet if the church decided an exorcism was necessary, few bishops would know of an exorcist to contact.

Only approved priests have performed exorcisms since the 1970s, but the church still includes elements of the ancient rite in some of its rituals. These rituals, according to Harak, include "a standard, prebaptismal ritual [containing] 'three scrutinies that are really rites of exorcism that have been kind of tamed in the church.' "[3]

The very fact that Cardinal O'Connor discussed exorcism in public is a testimony to the growing problem of demonism. Yet why are there so few exorcisms in the Roman Catholic Church and so few bishops who even know of an exorcist? Francis MacNutt writes that if a Roman Catholic is in need of an exorcism, too often he or she is referred to a psychiatrist.[4] Yet how can a psychiatrist or clinical psychologist diagnose a client as demonized when the profession has no diagnostic tools for such a condition, and in general disbelieves the existence of demons? Some changes in attitude are emerging, however.

Fathers Matthew and Dennis Linn report on a five-day retreat for one hundred Catholic priests. A psychiatrist was invited to teach on deliverance ministries. He told the priests that his patients needed their help through confession, prayer for healing of memories, and especially through loving deliverance when it is required. This same psychiatrist had publically stated just three years earlier that he had never seen a need for deliverance among his clientele.

As the destructive work of Satan has spread, the number of victims in need of help and healing has outstripped the number of professionals available to respond. The ministry of healing and deliverance is coming into the hands of the laity. People who have never been professionally trained are responding to the overwhelming need, and in simple faith are reaching out to God and His Word for guidance in ministering to these victims. It is for such people that I have written this book.

A PRIMER ON DELIVERANCE

Members of a specialized field of knowledge are often guilty of using jargon that is familiar to them but unknown to those outside the field. Since I want to make deliverance and exorcism clear to laypersons, it's time for me to present some short definitions of terms.

Professionals and lay Christians do not agree on all the theological fine points regarding the controversial subject of exorcism. I recognize that committed, Bible-believing Christians may differ with me on some points. Rather than confuse the reader with theological debate, however, I will simply give my best understanding of the meaning of these terms, based on my reading of Scripture and my professional experience.

Exorcist: A Christian who exercises the authority of Jesus Christ and the power of the Holy Spirit to cast out demons.

Exorcism: The healing process in which demonic spirits are bound and cast out in Jesus' name. This includes the healing of the inner emotional and mental wounds connected with demonic spirits. This is not a formal rite of the church, although it may at times have some formal or ritualized elements in it.

Inner Healing: An integral part of exorcism, the extended counseling and prayer needed to release and heal the emotional wounds of the past. It includes confession of sin, receiving God's forgiveness and cleansing, and the process of forgiving those who have injured the victim. Inner healing may extend for years beyond the formal exorcism events. I estimate that I spend 75 percent of my time talking and praying with victims in an inner healing ministry, and 25 percent in direct exorcism.

Deliverance: A term used synonymously with exorcism by most people. Some think of deliverance as a more general and informal process of prayer for release from demonic oppression, while exorcism is a more formalized encounter and personal battle with specific demon entities.

Demon Oppression: A demonic attack from without upon a person's mind or emotions. The demonic spirits do not indwell the person, but influence him or her strongly from outside. Depression, intense anxiety, or rage can be forms of demonic oppression, although they can also arise from other, nondemonic causes.

Demon Possession: The presence of a demon or demons within the personality structure of an individual. Possession is almost always partial in that the demons have some measure of control over mind, emotions, will, spirit, or flesh, but not total control. A person possessed by demons will almost certainly have some measure of control over her or his own actions and emotions. (There is legitimate theological debate concerning whether a Christian can be possessed by a demon. Some of the differences, in opinion, may be merely semantic. However, based on my experience in the field, I am convinced that demons can and do possess Christians, and that it occurs more often than people realize.)

Strong Man: The principal demon in a cluster or group of demons inhabiting a demonized person. This term is derived from Jesus' words in Mark 3:27, "No one can enter a strong man's house and plunder his goods, unless he first binds the strong man, and then he will plunder his house." It is helpful in an exorcism to identify this ruling demon, because when he is cast out, lesser demons frequently leave with him. The strong man will often be associated with powerful emotional traumas in someone's past that result in such disorders as deep rejection or a forceful present drive toward suicide.

Principality: This is the term for a demon that is even higher in Satan's authority structure than the strong man. Principalities are demons that rule over whole geographic areas, such as cities or even countries. Ephesians 6:12 says that "we do not wrestle against flesh and blood, but against principalities, against powers, against the rulers of the darkness of this age, against spiritual hosts of wickedness in the heavenly places." Strong men demons are under the authority of principalities, and in turn have powerful demons answering to them.

Anointing: A term some Christians use to refer to the power of the Holy Spirit acting through them in special or unusual situations. This special power enables a Christian to be particularly effective or insightful in a variety of areas of ministry, as, for example, very dynamic preaching. The anointing of the Holy Spirit in exorcism supplies the faith, authority, power, and knowledge needed to confront demonic forces.

Binding or Rebuking Evil Spirits: Exercising the authority Jesus gave to His church in Matthew 16:19, when He said to Peter: "I will give you the keys of the kingdom of heaven, and whatever you bind on earth will be bound in heaven." When an exorcist says to a demon, "I bind you in the name of Jesus," he means that, by the authority of Jesus, the demon is refused permission to further act, operate, or exercise influence over the person, place, or situation. Rebuking a demon means to check or restrain him by command, refusing to allow him to operate or sending him back to his rightful place in the bottomless pit.

Sealing with the Blood of Jesus: This phrase means that we ask God to place a protective covering over a person or place. This protection was purchased for Christians by the death and resurrection of Jesus. Thus we often pray or speak of "sealing" or "covering" with the blood of Jesus. That blood represents the life and death of Jesus, which purchased our salvation and protection. Through the efficacy of His shed blood we can approach God and claim His help against the demonic forces waging war against us. Satan hates to be reminded of the blood of Jesus and what it did for us. That is why satanists try to contaminate the symbol of blood to make it abhorrent.

DOORWAYS FOR DEMONS

There are many avenues through which demonic forces can gain entrance to individuals' lives. Sometimes through actual or implied invitation people actually give Satan and his demons a legal right to enter them. Satan is a legalist, and he will seize and enforce any opportunities given him to enter and control. In other cases people leave the doors of their lives "unlocked," so to speak, and demons are able to sneak in unnoticed. For others factors outside a person's control can make him or her vulnerable to demon oppression or possession.

A Pact with the Devil

The most obvious way for Satan to enter and control a person's life is to be legally invited to do so. We have discussed at length the practices of satanists, who, for the sake of power and present gain, give their eternal future to Satan. Pacts signed in their own blood allow powerful demons to enter them and exercise great control. One woman told me that in a satanic ritual she received a very strong demon of power to rule in her. When this demon entered her, she said, it was like being filled with liquid fire and incredible pain.

Occult Practices

As we have seen in earlier chapters, it doesn't necessarily take an outright pact with Satan to give demons access to a person's life. Any involvement, even on a superficial level, with occult practices can make a person vulnerable to demons. I have dealt with many cases in which the initial entrance of a demon could be traced to a childhood experience with a Ouija board, a seance, or another occult practice engaged in only once. And the longer occult practices continue, the more likely that possession will result.

Personal Sin

Continuing sin in a person's life can also create openings for demons. Certainly no Christian is perfect or sinless, and committing sin is not equivalent to becoming possessed. But when sin is repeated, encouraged, and unrepented, it can lead to demonization. Certain types of sin seem to be particularly attractive to demons.

For example, demonization has often been found in association with drug or alcohol abuse. The personality changes noted in many alcoholics can be due to demonic spirits' taking temporary control of their "host." As drunkenness progresses, often the eyes change in appearance and a rage and violence come out that were not there when the alcoholic was sober.

Cravings for pornography, as well as sins of lust and sexual perversion in general, are often associated with demons. Whenever there is an obsessive or addictive quality to a particular sin, demon activity can be suspected.

Family History

We've discussed in previous chapters the tragic cases of children born into families who have worshiped Satan for generations. It is almost impossible for the children in these families to escape being invaded by demons. These children may have been dedicated to Satan, even before they were born, and in those tender and vulnerable childhood years are unable to protect themselves from invading demons. Some of these families have even had curses on them that were passed down from generation to generation. Demonic spirits of witchcraft, sexual perversion, and suicide can be manifested at early ages in children whose family histories reveal the same problems in previous generations.

It is important for the descendants of families who have passed sin from one generation to another to confess and renounce any sin tendencies, bondages, or curses from the families' past. In Leviticus 26:40 God instructed the Israelites to "confess their sins and the sins of their fathers" even if they had not personally committed the same sins. And Daniel, a righteous man, in Daniel 9:20, prayed that he was "confessing my sin and the sin of my people Israel," even though he was not personally accountable for the sins of the Israelites. This kind of confession is, first of all, very cleansing and freeing. It is an open declaration to oneself, one's fellow believers, and particularly the demonic realm that you are renouncing any previous or familial attachments to Satan, and all of their curses and benefits. This confession is a commitment to walk with God in obedience and renounce the left-hand path.

Early Wounds or Traumas

It is sad but true that we are often most vulnerable to Satan in the places of our wounds and traumas. It is when we are in the middle of our pain that Satan takes advantage of us. Deeply traumatic experiences can open children to the tormenting spirits of fear, rage, or bitterness. Sometimes deep rejection begins even in the womb, as for instance, when an abortion is attempted but unsuccessful.

In a ministry of inner healing, I have often discovered demons hiding behind the deeply wounded emotions of a victim of trauma. Because the emotions are so strong, the focus of attention is on these intense feelings, and consequently, the presence of a demonic entity within can go undetected. Demons can hide behind these feelings, exercising influence and control and empowering self-destructive behaviors. I believe that those who minister in inner healing need to extend their ministry beyond prayer and counseling and be willing to be exorcists as well.

WARNING SIGNS: A PARENT'S GUIDE

Because satanism has targeted young people so intensely in the last decade, it is important for parents to be alert to signs in their children of demonic involvement. The teen years seem to be a time when children are especially vulnerable to the influences of the devil. The following is a list of important warning signs that parents should be aware of:

1. Extreme mood changes without any known precipitating cause (such as explosive rage with foul language)
2. Satanic symbols displayed on books or in notebooks (such as 666, Natas, an inverted cross, the pentagram,

a goat's head, the sign of the horn—a hand with the first and last fingers extended upward and the remainder folded down)

3. Withdrawing from family life
4. Heavy metal and black metal music
5. Listening for hours to this music
6. A dramatic change in clothing style (such as wearing all black with red accents)
7. Abusing drugs
8. Change in the peer group (such as leaving a more "normal" group to associate with a secretive group)
9. Staying out all night, especially on Friday night, at the time of the full moon, and on Satanist ceremonial days
10. Falling grades as well as many unexcused absences
11. Any sign of inhumanity to man or animals, such as cruelty, talking of blood, and a tendency toward macabre scenes
12. Beginning nightmares and a change in sleep patterns
13. Noticeable change in facial expression, especially in the eyes in times of rage

Obviously some of these symptoms taken alone, such as fluctuating grades or distancing from family, may simply represent developmental changes and normal ups and downs of the teen years. Parents should look for patterns in every area of a young person's life, not occasional differences. Of course, even if heavy metal music or satanic themes are found, possession may not have occurred. These are important warning signs, however, that the influence of demons in your child's life must be considered as a possibility. No parent wants to believe that a beloved child could be indwelt by demons, so the temptation for denial is strong. But it is much better to face reality and find release, than to relegate the works of Satan to fiction or to assume "it can't happen to my child."

HOW DO DEMONS ENTER?

I think that no one actually knows how a spiritual being, such as a demon, can enter a person's physical body. But we know that sin, occult involvement, and traumatic wounds are the kinds of doorways that spirits use to gain access to the personality or soul. People who have been demonized have testified to intense physical sensations associated with demons, such as a fiery burning sensation, pressure on the chest, a choking sensation, or intense nausea. However, this does not tell us anything about points of entry or specific locations of demons. We will have to be satisfied, in this life, to be left with a certain amount of mystery about the demonic realm and its processes of interaction with human beings.

CAN CHRISTIANS HAVE DEMONS?

As I mentioned earlier, there is considerable debate among Bible believers as to whether one who is a born-again Christian can also be demon possessed. Many say it is impossible, and they are adamant in their view. I respect the sincerity of other Christians' views in all matters; however, I have come to have a strong conviction that indeed demons can indwell Christians.

When we yield ourselves to Jesus, we begin new lives, and as with our physical lives, we begin our spiritual lives as babies. Daily we die to our flesh so the new persons we are in Christ can come forth for that day. No one can naturally and instantly begin to live a new life in Christ that is perfect; much has to die in us. We still sin, and we are still subject to the influence of the god of this world, Satan.

From my experiences in exorcism, I know Christians can have demons. Most of my clients have been born-again Christians. If these people have been taught that Christians

cannot be possessed, and they then discover they have demons inside themselves, the anguish and confusion are tormenting. They question whether they are really Christian.
Sometimes they go into denial, refusing to believe they
could be demonized, and abort the healing process before
it is complete.

If Christians can still sin—and we know that not only
can Christians sin, they do, in spite of their commitments
to follow Christ in all ways—it follows that sin in a Christian's life makes doorways that Satan can use to enter their
lives. In Ephesians 4:26–27, the apostle Paul says, "If you
are angry, don't sin by nursing your grudge. Don't let the
sun go down with you still angry . . . for *when you are
angry you give a mighty foothold to the devil*" (TLB, italics
added). The "mighty foothold" is a doorway Satan can use
to enter and possess a Christian as well as a non-Christian.

One of Satan's most effective tools, in my opinion, is the
common idea that Christians can't be demon possessed,
because those Christians who are demonized won't seek
healing and freedom.

THE CALLING OF AN EXORCIST

People argue about whether the ministry of exorcism is a
special calling of God or a special gift of the Holy Spirit. C.
Peter Wagner, in his book *Your Spiritual Gifts,* defines exorcism as a gift of the Holy Spirit. He says it is a gift, "the
special ability that God has given to certain members of the
Body of Christ to cast out demons and evil spirits."[5]

I also believe that exorcism is a call from God and a gift
of the Holy Spirit. Without the power and anointing of the
Spirit, I would never attempt exorcism. However, I don't
believe that God intended to make this an exclusive club. I
think He has called many to this ministry, but few have
been open to His call.

In Jesus' last words to His followers before He ascended into heaven, He emphasized that ordinary believers should use His authority to cast out demons and lay hands on the sick for healing. He said, "And those who believe shall use my authority to cast out demons, and they shall speak new languages. They will be able even to handle snakes with safety, and if they drink anything poisonous, it won't hurt them; and they will be able to place their hands on the sick and heal them" (Mark 16:17–18, TLB).

More members of the Body of Christ must be willing to enter into this life-saving ministry of healing the brokenhearted and setting the captives free. But it must be done with care. Never should novices engage powerful demons without help and without training.

The purpose of this book is to provide some guidelines for lay Christians in deliverance ministries, but those who feel called to such service should also find a competent exorcist who can train them and give them support. As you will see in the chapters to come, exorcism is best performed as a team ministry. There is no place in this kind of ministry for overconfidence or underpreparedness. It is a serious and demanding ministry and should not be entered into lightly or without the direction, empowering, and anointing of the Holy Spirit.

> My brethren, be strong in the Lord and in the power of His might. Put on the whole armor of God, that you may be able to stand against the wiles of the devil. For we do not wrestle against flesh and blood, but against principalities, against powers, against the rulers of the darkness of this age, against spiritual hosts of wickedness in the heavenly places. Therefore take up the whole armor of God, that you may be able to withstand in the evil day, and having done all, to stand.
>
> (Eph. 6:10–13)

9

PREPARING FOR EXORCISM

Do not give the devil a foothold.

(Eph. 4:27)

ONE OF THE most challenging aspects of an exorcism ministry is making a diagnosis. Distressed people seeking help often have tangled histories of mental and emotional problems. Unraveling the causes of their symptoms and deciding if they are due to physical, psychological, or spiritual problems or to demonic forces is a delicate process.

John White, psychiatrist and minister, explains the difficulty of this process and describes the overlapping of his two professions in dealing with patients who are under demonic influence.

As a psychiatrist I am as much a scientist as an artist. I am trained to skeptically examine hypotheses and to subject them to experiment. But the scientific method, limited enough in dealing even with material realities, collapses altogether in the face of the nonmaterial. To deal with demons I must know that they exist and I must also know that they are a factor in Joe Smith's disease. No scientific experiment could be devised to demonstrate conclusively the presence of Joe Smith's demon. Evidence, yes; proof, never.

You cannot exorcise demons you do not believe in. I am, therefore, obliged in the office to make a long stride where the occult is involved. The objective skeptical scientist must step across a chasm and believe.[1]

Based on traditional and generally accepted psychiatric and psychological diagnostic techniques, there is no way to reach a diagnosis of demon possession. The closest we can come is to make a diagnosis of multiple personality disorder. This is a diagnosis that an individual has had a "splitting off," usually because of traumatic circumstances, and formed one or more other personalities. Each personality is a part of the individual. However, for the individual who is demon possessed, multiple personality disorder does not adequately describe the condition. Some people who have experienced extreme traumas, such as victims of ritual abuse, for example, do form multiple personalities, and very often these victims are also indwelt by demons. But the demons are not merely additional personalities, for as R. D. Laing, a noted psychotherapist, says, "The individual seems to be the vehicle of a personality that is not his own. Someone else's personality seems to possess him."[2] (Please refer to Chapter 13 for a more indepth discussion of the implications of multiple personality disorder.)

J. L. Nevius has identified the characteristics of demon possession, an insight he gained from interviews with a number of missionaries on the field in China. Many of these missionaries were convinced they had dealt with a number of demonized people. These characteristics, which Nevius discusses in his book *Demon Possession,* are clearly different from the characteristics of multiple personality disorder.

1. The chief differentiating mark of a demon presence [from the presence of multiple personalities] is the persistent and consistent acting out of a new personality:

    a. The new personality says he is a demon.
    b. He/she uses personal pronouns: first person for him-
        self (the demon) and third person for the demonized
        person.
    c. The demon uses titles or names to refer to himself.
    d. The demon has sentient facial expressions and phys-
        ical manifestations that harmonize with his names
        and titles.
2. The demon gives evidence of knowledge and intellec-
    tual power unknown to the demonized person.
3. With the change of personality, there is a correspond-
    ing and dramatic change of moral character: aversion
    and hatred toward God and especially toward Christ.[3]

The difficulty of determining whether a client is suffering multiple personality disorder or another psychological
disorder and/or is in fact demon possessed is further complicated by the varying conditions that could cause him or
her to seek help from a minister or therapist.

1. The individual has severe emotional problems, but is
    not demonized.
2. The individual is psychotic, but is not demonized.
3. The individual is only oppressed by demons, but is not
    otherwise suffering emotional problems or psychotic.
4. The individual is demon possessed, but neither psy-
    chotic nor otherwise emotionally disturbed.
5. The individual has severe emotional problems and is de-
    monized.
6. The individual is both psychotic and demonized.
7. The individual is perfectly sane but is heavily involved
    in satanism, witchcraft, or other occult practices and,
    therefore, most likely is demonized.

It is important to consider from the outset whether there
could be physical causes for aberrant or unusual behavior

and symptoms. For example, demons can cause a person to have seizures, but a person can also have seizures that are caused by epilepsy. Therefore, if a client is having seizures, I recommend a complete neurological workup to discover if epilepsy or other problems are present before beginning treatment. In the absence of physical causes, I begin to suspect demons.

THE CASE HISTORY

A thorough personal history provides clues to the possibility of a demonic presence. In addition to social and medical background questions, a complete history should include questions about these areas.

1. As much information as possible concerning the parents' relationship, especially around the time of the client's conception and gestation. Was there rejection? Did the mother have serious emotional or physical problems? Were there any complications at birth?
2. The emotional climate of the family. What emotional hurts did the client encounter growing up in the family or at school? Was the family angry, abusive, calm, distant?
3. History of previous generations. Did any ancestors have unusual deaths, sicknesses, suicides, murders, or alcoholism? Was there any occult involvement?
4. Personal history. Has the client ever used a Ouija board, followed astrology, seen a psychic or medium? Is there any problem with alcohol or drug abuse?

I also probe the client's reactions to coming for our first appointment. I encourage him or her to be aware of what is going on inside. Very often a person will say, "Well, don't be offended, but there were thoughts in my head about coming here, like 'Don't go to Dr. Olson. He can't help you. Stay away from him.'" Often clients experience a real struggle coming to my office for a second appointment. Sometimes they get lost along the way or come on the wrong day. These struggles are valuable indicators of the presence of demons, for I believe I am known in the spirit world.

On several occasions I have been astonished that the demons in a person knew me and knew what to expect, even before I spoke with the person. For example, a missionary from Africa called and asked me to visit his son who was in a private psychiatric hospital receiving treatment for a drug problem. The father revealed that the son had been involved in witchcraft and satanism as well. As I walked down the hospital corridor, I could see the young man standing outside his room waiting for me. When I introduced myself, he gave me a knowing smile and said, "They know who you are."

I believe this prior knowledge of me on the part of the demons that are oppressing or possessing a person accounts for the tremendous struggle many people have when they want to seek help, and the difficulties they have returning for a second appointment.

SIGNS AND SYMPTOMS OF DEMONIC POSSESSION

It is easy to slip into a mentality in which one sees demons as the cause for everything from arthritis to insomnia, and chronic lower back pain to hypertension. Therefore, an exorcist cannot afford to jump to conclusions about the presence of demons. A careful therapist will probe all the physical and emotional evidence before entertaining the possibility. Since the suggestion of demonization is very traumatic for a client, it is important to be very convinced before suggesting the possibility.

Demonic manifestations are often characterized by their excessive nature, a feature that can help to differentiate them from normal emotional reactions. The client's history and present condition must be carefully evaluated to determine that these manifestations are present.

Christian Symbols and Sacraments

Demons within a person often react violently to the name of Jesus, the crucifix, Holy Communion, or being blessed with holy water or anointed oil. Reaction to Holy Communion is an especially powerful indicator of a demonic presence. Demons hate the blood of Christ represented by the bread and wine. As a demonized person watches or participates in a communion service, very often he or she experiences churning emotions and upsetting feelings or thoughts of blasphemy toward God or Christ.

Emotional Excess

A demonized person may exhibit excessive or uncontrollable rage, anger, and hate and/or excessive fear, guilt, and depression. There may be violent mood swings with no rational basis; a sudden depression may occur that is so deep it prompts suicidal thoughts.

A lack of control may be manifested in obsessions—repeated, intrusive thoughts that a person can neither reject nor control—or compulsions—powerful repetitive actions that he or she can't stop. The central issue concerning obsessions and compulsions is empowerment, for these behaviors can suggest a powerful driving force that is separate from the core personality and seeks to control the mind and will of the person.

This lack of self-control can be very frightening. Coupled with this "driven" feeling often there is a corresponding inability to love, forgive, or show normal emotions such as laughter and joy.

Impaired Thought Processes

At times demonized persons may experience a dazed state of consciousness, which they often describe as being like a hypnotic trance. Memory impairment is also present

in many people I have seen. They may have acted violently
but afterward have no memory of the incident. Often a client will complain that reading the Bible is too difficult and
when he does read it, it makes no sense to him. Other
thoughts may become muddled or confused.

Physical Symptoms

Demons also express themselves through physical symptoms. The eyes are said to be the window of the soul, and it
is quite true of those who are demonized. I have often
noted a change in the eyes of my clients when demons are
present. They can take on a deep darkness or a glazed look.
Sometimes the eyes have a wild look with a fiery yellow or
red glow from within.

A person who is demonized may also exhibit unbelievable strength. Some victims report a heaviness in the chest,
as if something were sitting there, making it hard to
breathe. Others say there are times when their throats close
and a choking sensation becomes very strong.

Sometimes there is a physical basis for these symptoms,
so a physician may need to be consulted. I worked with a
woman who complained of severe chest pains. Knowing
she had a history of heart surgery and coronary problems, I
referred her to the hospital for tests, but when the test
results came back, no physical basis for the pain was indicated. In a later session, we took authority over a demonic
spirit, and when it was cast out, she felt immediate relief.

PREPARATION FOR EXORCISM

Thorough preparation of a demonized person for inner
healing and exorcism is essential. Without adequate trust,
teaching, and spiritual cleansing beforehand, an exorcism
can be a traumatic and potentially harmful experience for
everyone involved. First there must be trust, spirituality,
and confession.

Developing Trust

Building a relationship with a client is a time-consuming process. The people I work with need to get to know and understand me and feel my sense of commitment to them. They need reassurance that I will not abandon them before their healing is complete. And they need to be sure that my ministry is legitimate and scriptural before they place themselves in my care. For these reasons, I do not rush through the process of taking case histories and assessing a person's areas of woundedness and need. During this time I explain thoroughly the role each of us will play in the healing process.

Spiritual Preparedness

A successful exorcism is impossible unless there is an unconditional commitment to Jesus Christ. If someone comes to see me who is not a Christian, I will do everything I can to lead that person into a saving relationship with Jesus first, for in an exorcism, there is no neutral ground. One is either for Christ or for Satan. I will not put myself or someone else through an exorcism that cannot possibly succeed.

Once I am certain that my client is truly born again in Christ, I discuss the need for prayer, the reading of God's Word, and worship, and I use Scripture to teach clearly and emphatically the authority of the believer over Satan.

Unconfessed Sin

Since sin is one doorway through which Satan can gain access to a believer, it is essential that sin is thoroughly renounced, confessed, and forgiven. As I probe for potentially harmful sin areas, I ask questions such as:

- Have you ever had an abortion? Did you confess it and receive God's forgiveness?

- If there has been occult involvement, have you confessed it and asked forgiveness?
- Are you currently involved in an illicit sexual relationship? Are you willing to break it off?
- Are there any matters still on your conscience that are nagging at you and making you feel guilty? If so, let us confess them now and receive God's forgiveness.
- Is there any person whom you have wronged? Do you need to make restitution? Has that person forgiven you?

INNER HEALING

The majority of people I serve are victims of someone else's cruelty and brutality. Because they need deep inner healing for damaged emotions and painful memories, the central question that must be asked is, "How have you reacted to this painful trauma that was inflicted on you?"

Anger and Depression

When a person is deeply hurt, anger is a natural response. There are two ways of handling the anger: The victim can express it or suppress it. Anger expressed inappropriately or sinfully can harden into rage, hatred, and vengeful impulses. Suppressed anger, on the other hand, becomes depression. If anger is never dealt with appropriately, in time the victim becomes bitter, resentful, and consumed by it. Thus the sin committed against the person prompts his or her own sin, as the person responds wrongly to the tormentors.

Each of us has been hurt by others, and we react to those hurts in anger. But you and I are responsible for our actions and our choices and God holds us accountable. You may say, "I didn't choose to feel rage, resentment, bitterness, and hate," but on closer examination, one must see that these reactions are personal decisions. Although for victims of brutality these reactions may be very difficult to give up, with Christ's grace it is possible.

The apostle Paul instructs us to "get rid of all bitterness, rage and anger, brawling and slander, along with every form of malice. Be kind and compassionate to one another, forgiving each other, just as in Christ God forgave you" (Eph. 4:31–32).

Many of my clients struggle with the issue of forgiveness. Having been victims of unutterable horrors, they find it nearly impossible to overcome the hate they feel inside. I try to impress on them these key truths:

- You victimize yourself by dwelling on what was done to you and becoming resentful, bitter, and hateful.
- Hate is the means by which we punish and destroy ourselves because of the actions of others.
- As you continue to hate, you continue to give your enemy power over you.
- When you are filled with bitterness and hate, it does not change the other person or what happened to you. It only magnifies it and blocks God's healing in your life.

The sin of bitterness destroys individuals, families, and churches. No matter how difficult it is, forgiveness is the only way out of a dead-end situation, for repentance, confession, and absolution are the road to freedom.

Inner Vows

When people are wounded, they often respond by making inner vows. These vows are promises we make to ourselves that limit and control our future behavior. For example, a young girl is molested by her father. She may make an inner vow, "I will never trust a man again." She will then limit her future, perhaps by being unable to sustain a marriage relationship or by refusing to have any relationships with men. Or she could reach a different conclusion and make a different kind of vow, saying, "God allowed this pain to happen to me. I am furious with Him! I will never trust Him again!" This is an inner vow that can affect her not only for the rest of her lifetime, but for eternity!

People make inner vows about their emotions and their actions: "I will never forgive him." "I'll get even some day." "I'll never speak to her again." "I'll never be able to get over this." "I'll never allow myself to be vulnerable again."

When I take a personal history and probe wounded areas, I always try to discover if the client has made any inner vows. And I always lead my clients in prayer to renounce and release the vows they have made. They need to regain their freedom to act and react in the present instead of being bound by the past.

Healing

Even the Holy Spirit respects a person's free will, and He will not violate an inner vow of unforgiveness or bitterness. It is up to each of us to release those vows and freely invite Him in to do His healing work. Once sins have been confessed and vows renounced or broken, then the Holy Spirit is free to heal the damaged areas within. And demons that have been attached to those areas of a person have to leave. They no longer have a legal right to remain in that person's life.

One woman who finally broke free of this bondage told me, "My inner vow was that I would never love a man like my father—and yet, men like him were the only kind I attracted." Bitter vows attract bitter people—and that doesn't sound like a good way to live!

THE DEMANDS OF EXORCISM

As you work in this ministry area, you quickly discover that inner healing and exorcism are the most confrontive and demanding experiences a person can face. As C. S. Lewis once said, "There is no neutral ground in the universe; every square inch, every split second is claimed by God and counterclaimed by Satan."[4] Sin must be taken very seriously. In a life-and-death battle with Satan, he will not give an inch, and neither can we.

Preparing Yourself

It is as important for the exorcist to be free of sin and clean before God as for the demonized person. On an ongoing basis, I begin each day by putting on the helmet of salvation, the shield of faith, and the breastplate of righteousness referred to in Ephesians 6. I use the sword of the Spirit, which is the Word of God, to examine my life and prepare me for battle. I want to be certain that there are no sin issues between me and God that would block the flow of the Holy Spirit in the exorcism and healing process.

If an exorcist is haphazard or superficial in preparing a demonized person or himself for the experience of exorcism, he places both himself and his client in jeopardy. Satan is serious about keeping his victims in bondage, and we must be equally serious about setting them free.

10

ANATOMY OF AN EXORCISM

He gave them power over unclean spirits,
to cast them out, and to heal all kinds of
sickness.

(Matt. 10:1)

NO TWO EXORCISMS are exactly alike. A complex mixture of ingredients affects the length, intensity, and character of the battle. The background of the demonized person and his or her history of trauma, the depth of involvement with Satan, the person's present emotional stability, the level of determination to be set free, the identity of the strong man, and the number of demons present all affect the process of exorcism. And exorcism is just that: a process. It can be relatively brief and painless, but this is the exception. Most exorcisms take many hours, but they can also take several days, weeks, or, in extreme cases, even years for the healing to be complete and the demons cast out.

PREPARING FOR BATTLE

An exorcism is truly a life-and-death struggle, so it is important to engage the enemy with every advantage you can muster. Satan will use all available devices to frighten his victim and intimidate the team into quitting. I try to create a time and a setting that will strengthen the exorcism team and encourage and sustain the will of the demonized person.

Place: If at all possible, a church building is the preferred place. One of my favorite spots was a small but beautiful chapel that I was permitted to use for a time. It had a quiet, gentle atmosphere and an uplifting sense of God's presence. If a church isn't available, I use my home or office. I have a tape recorder so I can play praise music, creating a worshipful environment.

Time: I prefer to work during daylight hours. Satan is the prince of darkness, and it is easier to feel oppressed by him at night. For most people, daytime is when they feel most energized, and there is a greater sense of safety in the daylight.

Fasting: In some cases, it may help to fast and pray before an exorcism. Jesus spoke to His apostles of a demon that would not come out "except by prayer and fasting" (Matt. 17:21). I don't fast just prior to an exorcism, however. I find that I need food, especially protein, for energy, for this is hard work. It is very exhausting and requires an optimum physical condition.

The Team: It is best to have Christians who understand the power of the Holy Spirit working as a team in an exorcism. From just the physical point of view, it helps to have other people to hold the subject when a demonic spirit is fighting. The more powerful demons, which often control people who have been deeply involved in witchcraft and satanism, can be incredibly strong.

It is also important that the team have a designated

leader so that everyone isn't speaking at the same time. A team of people praying loudly can be very disconcerting and disruptive. Team members should know one another, communicate well, and have confidence in each other.

As an experienced exorcist, I have often worked alone. People with jobs and families can't always make themselves available for an exorcism lasting several days or weeks. If the needs of the client are critical and no team is available, I will work with him or her by myself.

Intercessors: I have been blessed with people who pray for me. God has put it on the heart of a Phoenix woman to intercede for me daily. Also a group in Wyoming gives me regular prayer support. When I need additional prayer warriors, I call and ask for help. If any readers want to include me and my family in their prayers for protection and God's power, I'd deeply appreciate it.

THE TOOLS OF AN EXORCIST

Certain aids are essential to the exorcist. First among these is the Word of God, His love for the victim, and the authority of the name of Jesus. Christian symbols—such as a crucifix, holy water, or anointing oil—and sacraments— like Holy Communion—are also powerful in combating the enemy.

The Word of God

The Word of God is the sword of the Spirit and plays a central role in exorcism. Scripture is used both in preparing the demonized person to understand His authority, and in enforcing that authority on the demons during the exorcism. I emphasize passages like the following:

> When Jesus had called the Twelve together, he gave them power and authority to drive out all demons and to cure

diseases, and he sent them out to preach the kingdom of
God and to heal the sick.

(Luke 9:1–2)

I have given you authority to trample on snakes and scorpions and to overcome all the power of the enemy; nothing
will harm you.

(Luke 10:19)

And these signs will accompany those who believe: In
my name they will drive out demons.

(Mark 16:17)

Whatever you bind on earth will be bound in heaven,
and whatever you loose on earth will be loosed in heaven.

(Matt. 18:18)

Though we live in the world, we do not wage war as the
world does. The weapons we fight with are not the weapons of the world. On the contrary, they have divine power
to demolish strongholds.

(2 Cor. 10:3–4)

The Love of God

It is important to realize that authority and power over
Satan are not produced by loudly shouting for demons to
leave; authority and power are grounded in the victory of
Jesus Christ over Satan and the bestowal of His authority on
us as believers.

It is easy to get carried away in the heat of the battle.
Insensitive exorcists have been known to infect the person
being delivered with fear, to the point of terrorizing him or
her. Exorcists who spend hours shouting and screaming at
demons to depart can leave the vulnerable person they are
trying to help traumatized and wounded. Emotionalism,
shouting, or any physical abuse against the victim must be
strictly avoided. Demons do not leave because of the

actions of our carnal nature. They leave because we enforce the authority of Christ under the anointing of the Holy Spirit.

In a successful exorcism, the love of God is uppermost in the minds of the ministry team and can be felt by the person being set free. Kindness and gentleness, the laying on of hands in prayer for healing, and even a hug at appropriate times (with the permission of the client), can best express the unconditional love of God so needed by the suffering victim of Satan's cruelty.

God's love is the greatest gift of the Holy Spirit and is wonderful for healing. It enables a minister to accept and love a demonized person, and the ultimate victory is always because of the power of God's love in action.

Christian Symbols

I often use a crucifix in exorcism. Perhaps because of my Lutheran background, this symbol of Christ's victory is very meaningful to me, and I've discovered that Satan absolutely hates it. Demons don't like to look at the crucifix, and it seems to agitate them so much that they want to leave.

Holy water is another device that can be powerful in the battle. I pray over clean, fresh water, asking the Holy Spirit to bless it. I offer my client a glass of this water blessed by the Spirit, and demons react quickly. Often they will leave when it is consumed.

The more powerful the demons, the stronger their reactions will be to holy water, the crucifix, or anointing oil that has been blessed by the Holy Spirit. Demons sometimes recoil as if burned when touched by these holy objects.

Holy Communion

Again, my Lutheran background has given me a deep reverence for the sacrament of Holy Communion. I have seen its powerful effect for driving out demons, so I always have communion elements close at hand.

Communion dramatically reminds demons of the blood of Jesus which may be the most potent weapon there is against satanic agents. The Bible teaches us:

1. "The life of a creature is in the blood" (Lev. 17:11).
2. "Without the shedding of blood there is no forgiveness" (Heb. 9:22).
3. As our High Priest, Jesus' blood was shed so that once and for all an acceptable sacrifice was made for our salvation (see Heb. 9:11–15).
4. Jesus, our ransom, redeemed us and set us free from our sins with his precious blood (1 Peter 1:18–19).

When I give a chalice of wine representing the blood of Christ to a demonized person, I like to remind the demons that "the accuser of our brethren . . . has been cast down. And they overcame him by the blood of the Lamb and by the word of their testimony" (Rev. 12:10–11).

PREPARING THE SUBJECT

Before the exorcism begins, my instructions to my client are along these lines: "In the final analysis, you are your own exorcist. You have to take an active role by professing your faith in Jesus and using your authority to cast out demons in His name." I explain that fear is Satan's ultimate weapon, and the demons on the verge of departure will often use fear as a last-ditch effort to avoid defeat.

I often remember Brian as a young man who exemplified the right attitude of self-exorcism. He was in his thirties when he came to me and said, "I have demons in me, and I want them out. Jesus Christ is my Lord—so let's get on with it." I'll never forget the smile on his face every time a demon manifested his presence, because Brian knew it was leaving, and he could rejoice. He was set free in two visits.

Two Key Questions

I ask my client two key questions before we begin. First, "Do you want to be healed?" Most people will quickly say, "Yes."

The next question is perhaps more important: "Do you believe you can be healed?" There may be hesitation, doubt, guilt, and the fear that he or she is not worthy of being healed. It is important to deal with the problem of unworthiness before the exorcism begins.

Negative Self-image

As I listen to a client describe her childhood, I soon get clues of where a sense of unworthiness or a negative self-image may have originated. Demeaning, critical words of parents can be a curse on a child. When I discover negative words implanted from childhood, I pray to break the power of those words by the authority of Jesus. I ask Him to free the conscious and subconscious mind and release the memories and emotions from these demeaning words. Then we talk about the joy of having a God who loves the messed up, unworthy people of this world.

Physical Sensations

A demonized person should be prepared for the physical sensations that sometimes accompany an exorcism. There may be feelings of nausea and actual vomiting. Sometimes demons exit through a mass of phlegm or mucous expelled through the mouth. It helps to keep on hand some tissues, a clean, dry towel, and a wastebasket or pail, which we sometimes jokingly call a "demon bucket." In the midst of so serious a process, it's helpful to have some occasional comic relief.

I also explain that there may be sharp pains in the heart, head, or places where there was a physical injury in the past. Sometimes a strong choking sensation comes upon the victim. I ask him to let me know immediately of these things, and I anoint the area with oil and pray against the pain.

THE EXORCISM

Exorcism begins with a time of prayer. This is a sample of the kind of prayer I pray:

> I take authority in the name of Jesus Christ over this room and cast out all demons in this room. I seal this room with the blood of Jesus. I plead the blood of Jesus over every person in this room and in this neighborhood.
>
> I take authority over the demonic spirits in the air above this room and the ground beneath this office in the name of Jesus Christ. I bind all demons from hell that would come against us and refuse them entrance. In Jesus Christ's name I bind the forces of Satan in fire, water, and nature.
>
> I ask you, Heavenly Father, to send your warrior angels to do battle in the heavens and come against all the principalities and powers and rulers of darkness who would interfere with us. I also ask, Father, for warrior angels to come to this room to prevent violence from demonic spirits. Let angels link arms around this building, and prevent all communication and calls for help between demons in this person and demons in other places.

I know that angels protect and assist me. Recently a demon tried to kill a woman who had run out of my office and attempted to jump a second-story railing. As we raced to help, I feared we would find her body on the concrete below, but something had already intervened. She said with a tremble, "That was a powerful force that stopped me." Those angels' hands are huge!

Anointing for Healing

After prayer I anoint the demonized person's head with oil in the sign of the Cross in the name of the Father, Son, and Holy Spirit. I place my hands lightly on the head and pray for the anointing of the Holy Spirit for all present.

Since I know from previous interviews the areas of woundedness in the person's life, I begin to pray for inner healing of those memories and emotions. I accomplish as much inner healing as possible, because demons' claws can't attach to areas that are healed.

Binding the Strong Man

As I am praying, demons often begin to stir, so I keep checking with the person to see what is going on inside. I ask him to look in my eyes. I tell him that what I am about to say is not directed at him, but at the strong man, the ruling demon inside. Then I speak to the demon forces:

> I take authority in the name of Jesus Christ and bind the strong man within from the conscious mind of this person, from the subconscious mind, memories, spirit, and soul, and from the will and body. In the name of Jesus Christ I rebuke and pray against the influence of all ancestral demons from his mother's and father's families.

The eyes of a victim change when a demon manifests itself. They take on a wild, hateful look as I command the demon to look into my eyes for a confrontation. The war has begun.

Some exorcists believe in the importance of discovering the strong man's name. They command the demon within to name himself. The problem with this is that demons so often lie. The key to finding out which demon is most powerful in a person's life is to examine the emotional problems he has presented. Expect a demon of rejection for someone who has been wounded deeply by rejection. If a person is suicidal, bind and cast out demons of suicide, death, and self-destruction. If a subject has been sexually abused, no doubt there will be demonic spirits of lust, incest, sexual perversion, and shame. There may also be the spirit of fear—fear of men or women and fear of sex. In working with former satanists and witches, I have found that the strong man is very proud and will give his name.

Under each strong man there are other powerful demons that must be detected and cast out. I read aloud the authority Scriptures that I've used in preparing the client, such as Luke 10:19, Mark 16:17, and Matthew 16:19. The authority of the name of Jesus is powerful over Satan and his demons:

> Therefore God exalted him to the highest place and gave him the name that is above every name, that at the name of Jesus every knee should bow, in heaven and on earth, and under the earth, and every tongue confess that Jesus Christ is Lord, to the glory of God the Father.
>
> (Phil. 2:9–11)

These Scriptures, read after the strong man is bound, stop all the nonsense of demons saying, "You have no power to cast me out" or "You are not strong enough to make us leave." The passages reinforce the fact that we will not permit the demons to manipulate the exorcism or distract us from our goal of casting them out.

After binding the strong man demon and all his cohorts and reading the Scriptures on the believer's authority, it is usually an excellent time to administer Holy Communion.

Physical Pain

During inner healing or exorcism often the victim feels physical pain associated with the memories of abuse or injury, a phenomenon I call "body memories." The pain is very real to the victim, and it is necessary to anoint the areas of pain with oil in the sign of the Cross, asking the Father to erase those memories and stop the physical pain. Then I bind all demons associated with those memories.

How Demons Leave

Demons most often leave a person through coughing, coughing up phlegm, deep burping of gaslike bubbles, or screaming. But sometimes they leave silently. I check to see whether a victim's stomach is upset, and tell him not to hold back if it is. They most often have sensations of a presence in the stomach, which moves up the esophagus to the mouth. There are times when the demon blocks the throat, causing a choking sensation. I anoint the area with oil or put holy water in the person's mouth to break the hold of the demon. I may ask the person to say, "I cough you out in the name of Jesus Christ." This helps him or her to be less passive in the exorcism process. Sometimes demons will leave quietly with no manifestation of their departure. Some people have reported demonic spirits leaving through the fingertips, eyes, nose, and other parts of the body.

The Aftermath

After the demons have been expelled, the person feels exhausted. I pray for the infilling of the Holy Spirit and His healing presence. Although a number of demons have left and the person feels better, there may be, and often are, more demons remaining. In fact, it's usually the most powerful ones who stay behind. This time of peaceful rest may be the best time to end the session until another day. Because I have learned God was watching my clients long before I ever met them, I know I can trust Him to care for them until the next time.

Remember, inner healing and exorcism are a process that often takes repeated sessions. Prematurely claiming a complete victory "by faith" can be very damaging if all the demons are not truly gone. A good exorcist will be committed to see the process through until the end, no matter how many sessions it takes.

BLOCKS TO FREEDOM

Spirit entities do not react passively to our attempts to eject them. They will use any form of trickery or evasion they can to remain in hiding.

Games Demons Play

Demons often try to make their victims sleepy or passive or put them in a trancelike state. The spirit of passivity is a powerful, deceptive spirit, and I confront it strongly and cast it out quickly if I detect its presence.

There are times demons want to talk, to tell the exorcist, "You don't have enough power," and the like. I refuse to get involved with conversations with a demon, because it gives them the opportunity to manipulate the exorcism process.

Sometimes a powerful demon will put on a show of power with bizarre manifestations to try to impress, distract, or frighten the exorcist. The intent is to divert the team from the central purpose of casting out the demons. I take authority over this spirit and its games, and bind it from communicating with the realm of darkness outside, attempting to call in reinforcements.

Demons lie to their victims. They say that if they leave, the person will suffer terribly. They misuse Scriptures, such as the words of the apostle Paul, "I have been crucified with Christ" (Gal. 2:20), to frighten and confuse. They whisper, "If I leave, you will be nailed like Jesus was on a cross, so it is better to let me stay than for you to go on with God." Believe it or not, these encounters can be serious times of testing for victims. Although they will not endure a physical crucifixion, it is true that the Christian life is not an easy one and in it there is an element of cross bearing. The whisperings are times of challenge for victims to make deep commitments to God to go on with Him at any cost. I encourage them with Deuteronomy 30:19–20:

I call heaven and earth to witness against you that today I
have set before you life or death, blessing or curse. Oh, that
you would choose life; that you and your children might
live! Choose to love the Lord your God and to obey him and
to cling to him, for he is your life and the length of your
days. (TLB)

Other Problems

If everything has been tried and demons still refuse to
leave, it's important to go back over preparatory ground to
see if anything was missed. Demons may be able to maintain a foothold for these reasons:

- Unconfessed sin.
- Unrenounced occult activity.
- Unwillingness to surrender to the Lordship of Christ.
  For instance, a person with a demon of lust may be
  reluctant to give it up for fear of losing the passion of
  his or her sex life.
- Unforgiveness.
- Uncompleted inner healing of damaged emotions and
  memories.
- Inner vows that haven't been revealed and broken.
- Lack of faith. Faith is not a feeling of confidence that
  healing will take place, but a commitment of the will
  to believe God's Word that healing is indeed possible.
- Tacit agreements. A tacit agreement is a spoken or un-
  spoken statement that implies a legal contract with demonic forces. Satan is a legalist, and he will try to
  enforce any implied agreement. "I wish I was dead," is
  a tacit agreement with the spirit of death. "I just can't
  go on anymore," is a tacit agreement with the spirit of
  hopelessness and despair. "My life will never be any
  different," becomes a tacit agreement with the spirit of
  resignation. (I confront the person with these statements and ask him to renounce them in Jesus' name.)

- Failure of the exorcist to continue to victory. Some exorcists feel that after two or three sessions they have done all they can. They won't commit to spend whatever time is needed to complete the healing.
- Failure of the demonized person to break emotional ties to ungodly relationships of the past, such as former sexual partners or friends who are still involved in occult practices.

In general, it is good to check all the "doorways" to Satan listed in Chapter 8 to see if any access has been left open to demons to continue in or return to the victim's life.

STAYING FREE

During the process of healing, it is important for clients to read the Bible out loud at home, to play praise music, to receive Holy Communion daily, and to be regular worshipers at church. They need to surround themselves with the love and comfort of God. If at all possible, they should join a prayer and praise group in the church to encircle them with prayer and support.

When engaged in the process of exorcism, subjects must be prepared for attacks by demons trying to oppress and intimidate them. It is vital that they realize their own authority in Christ to command the demons to leave.

When a former victim of Satan goes through an exorcism, he or she may be freed but left defenseless, unstable, and subject to further demonic infestation. This is a time for spiritual growth in Christ. Prayer, worship, and fellowship with a Bible-believing group of Christians is essential.

Many people who have been set free from demons want to join the battle against Satan, but I believe a person is too vulnerable immediately after an exorcism. At least a year is needed to consolidate the victory and stabilize his or her life and Christian walk. After that time, if the person still feels led into the ministry, then he can find a qualified exorcist and join the team.

I just love to see the transformation in people's lives—their eyes shine, their faces glow, and there is a joy that comes from God, because, as the song says, "our God reigns." Jesus Christ has set the captives free, and again Satan is defeated! There is no satisfaction for an exorcist so great as the Spirit-filled life of a person set free to love and serve the Lord.

PART FOUR

FREEDOM

If the Son sets you free, you will be free
indeed.

(John 8:36)

11

TO HEAL AND SET FREE

The Spirit of the Lord GOD is upon Me,
Because the LORD has anointed Me
To preach good tidings to the poor;
He has sent Me to heal the brokenhearted,
To proclaim liberty to the captives,
And the opening of the prison to those who are bound;
To proclaim the acceptable year of the LORD.

(Isa. 61:1–2)

JESUS CAME TO do far more than teach and preach about the kingdom of God. He came to heal. The very name of Jesus means to heal, to save, and to make whole. Jesus proclaimed that the kingdom was demonstrated powerfully when He healed the sick and the brokenhearted and when He set captives free from their bondage to Satan.

I must confess that for most of my life as a pastor I did not see how central healing was in the ministry of Jesus and His disciples. Jesus intensively trained twelve men for three years to heal the sick, cast out demons, and proclaim the gospel of God's kingdom. In Mark 3:14–15 we read: "He appointed twelve—designating them apostles—that they might be with him and that he might send them out to preach *and to have authority to drive out demons*" (emphasis added). And Matthew 10:1 says: "He called his twelve disciples to him *and gave them authority to drive out evil spirits and to cure every kind of disease and sickness*" (emphasis added).

I don't know how many times I read these passages, yet the only thing I saw was that Jesus called twelve disciples and sent them out to preach. When I gave sermons on these texts, I touched only on evangelism. It wasn't until I became involved in exorcism that I finally listened to all the words of Jesus. I am certainly in no position to be critical of other pastors who suffer from the same selective perception that I did for so many years.

Discovering the Holy Spirit

Through the empowerment of the Holy Spirit, Jesus' present-day disciples have authority to heal and cast out demons, just as His disciples did two thousand years ago.

Jesus Himself received the power of the Holy Spirit when He was baptized at the river Jordan. John the Baptist said of Christ, "To him God gives the Spirit without limit" (John 3:34).

Before Jesus ascended to heaven, He reminded the disciples that He would send the Holy Spirit to fill them with power. At Pentecost the disciples were filled with the power of the Holy Spirit, just as Jesus had promised. And this same Spirit was promised to all future believers.

> Peter replied, "Repent and be baptized, every one of you, in the name of Jesus Christ so that your sins may be forgiven. And you will receive the gift of the Holy Spirit. The promise is for you and your children and for all who are far off—for all whom the Lord our God will call."
>
> (Acts 2:38–39)

We need not doubt that the same dynamic empowerment of the Holy Spirit is available to us today for ministry filled with signs and wonders, healing of the sick, and casting out demons.

When I try to bring about God's will on my own, I usually fail. The more I can get out of God's way, the more I become a usable vessel for the Holy Spirit's power to flow through me. I dare not depend on my own abilities to cast out demons or heal the brokenhearted.

INNER HEALING

The power of the Holy Spirit heals wounded memories and damaged emotions. People who need exorcism will invariably need inner healing as well. As damaged emotions and traumatic memories are touched by the great Healer, the process of demons taking their leave speeds up.

A part of the process of inner healing is the infilling of the Holy Spirit to enable the person to live daily a Christ-centered life. If this infilling does not take place, demons may return and cause more damage than before the exorcism. Jesus warned of this very thing:

> When an evil spirit comes out of a man, it goes through arid places seeking rest and does not find it. Then it says, "I will return to the house I left." When it arrives, it finds the house swept clean and put in order. Then it goes and takes seven other spirits more wicked than itself, and they go in and live there. And the final condition of that man is worse than the first.
>
> (Luke 11:24–26)

Beyond Psychotherapy

For years, as a clinical psychologist and pastoral counselor, I searched for keys to healing. Through psychotherapy I would probe, listen, and try to discover root causes for clients' problems and pain. I sought to share my insight with those I counseled, hoping the new understanding would bring them help and release. Unfortunately, I found that for many insight was simply not sufficient for healing. In fact in many cases it added new pain as formerly suppressed and denied memories overwhelmed the coping abilities of the client.

I have since discovered that the healing of these traumatic memories and damaged emotions is beautifully accomplished by the power of the Holy Spirit. "He heals the brokenhearted and binds up their wounds" (Ps. 147:3).

I have come to define inner healing as psychotherapy empowered by the Holy Spirit. I use all the skills and knowledge I have learned through clinical psychology to discover a client's root problems and present needs. When it comes time for healing, I pray for the Holy Spirit to produce the necessary healing. I never know how quickly He will work or in what ways He will minister to the wounded individual. Many times He surprises me.

A Typical Case

Years ago someone I'll call Steve came to me for counseling. In his early thirties, he was emotionally devastated. After ten years of marriage, his wife had asked him for a divorce. In anguish he poured out his confusion and pain.

"I thought we had a good Christian marriage; today she told me why she wants a divorce. She left me for another woman!"

Steve broke down weeping. I asked him if he would mind if I prayed for him, requesting the Lord to heal this deep wound of rejection. He agreed to let me pray.

"Lord, you know what rejection is all about," I prayed. "Please heal Steve's deep pain of rejection."

When I finished praying, I opened my eyes to find Steve smiling, though tears still streamed down his face. He was filled with an overwhelming peace.

"I can't believe what happened to me," Steve said. "Soon after you began to pray, I felt I was standing at the foot of the Cross. Jesus hung there, in such pain Himself. When He looked into my face and saw my pain, He ripped Himself from the Cross and came and put His arms around me. He healed my broken heart." Steve left a different man.

Healing the Inner Child

A woman I'll call Janet came to see me one April day, seeking inner healing. She reported that the previous January, during a conversation with a relative, she recalled some extremely painful memories of sexual abuse during her childhood. She had effectively blocked these memories for years, but once they surfaced, they were more than she could cope with.

From the age of five, Janet was sexually molested by a teenage boy her family had adopted. She was having difficulty sleeping because of recurring painful memories of the experiences. She simply couldn't turn off the constant stream of mental pictures of the horror.

As I began to pray with her, she experienced an emotional return to her five-year-old self. She began screaming as she did years before when being sexually attacked. I prayed a quick prayer. "Jesus, heal that hurting little girl inside Janet."

Instantly, Jesus healed her. When I saw her again the next week, Janet was filled with joy and said she felt like she was floating on a cloud. Again, I had witnessed the powerful ability of the Holy Spirit to heal instantly.

I've often reflected on these two dramatic healings. Certainly, one reason the Lord healed them so quickly may have been because of their intense pain and need. But I often wonder if there wasn't a second reason: to teach me that nothing is impossible for Him. During more involved and difficult cases of inner healing, the memories of former healing help me to not get discouraged. He is the one who heals; I am only the one who prays. Little did I realize at the time of these healings how much I still had to learn of perseverance and patience when healing would take far longer than one or two sessions.

HEALING AND THE SUBCONSCIOUS MIND

Inner healing seeks to deal with memories that may not be readily available to the conscious mind. Thus therapists look for ways to access the subconscious. One technique that is now used widely is called "visualization." This technique uses a client's imagination to create a mental picture or story. Christian therapists often ask clients to picture themselves in a beautiful or relaxing setting, perhaps a mountain meadow or a secluded beach. Then they suggest that the client introduce Jesus into the scene. The client can "see" Jesus sitting next to her, and begin to experience His love and acceptance. Or the therapist asks the client to relive a painful memory from the past, but to change the memory to include Jesus. Again, this method can bring healing to those painful memories.

When I first began to use inner healing, I employed visualization techniques. Since that time I have had to seriously rethink my position on visualization and an associated therapeutic technique, hypnosis. Having been trained in medical hypnosis, it was a natural for me to use this technique. However, my experience in dealing with the demonic has caused me to view hypnosis differently.

Some theorize that hypnosis bypasses the analytical functions of the left hemisphere of the brain, directly accessing the subconscious. Because I have seen how much Satan wants to have access to the subconscious mind to influence or control it, I have grave concerns about the passive state of mind induced by hypnosis and visualization. The relaxed, suggestible state of the client may, in my view, provide open doors for demonic presences.

One of the most strongly demonized clients I ever worked with was a woman who had been in hypnotherapy for a year and a half. Her therapist, whom I discovered was a truly evil man, used hypnosis to regress her to the age of five, and then raped her repeatedly. During her altered state of consciousness, induced through hypnosis, powerful demonic spirits entered her. The more often people allow themselves to be put in an altered state of consciousness, the more passive and suggestible they become.

I know that many Christian therapists teach visualization to aid their clients in inner healing. Most who use visualization do not see any connection with hypnosis. Yet the techniques are quite similar: total relaxation, deep breathing exercises, a soft, singsong voice directing the "visualization." All tend to place the subjects in a very passive state.

I am also concerned that the "Jesus" envisioned by clients could be a demonic deception. When people place too much emphasis on the imagined words of an imagined Jesus, they open themselves to possible imbalance, self-deception, and perhaps demonic deception. Satan is a master of masquerade, and if he can appear as an angel of light, he can easily impersonate Jesus. He could use the opportunity to give misleading guidance or false peace.

I urge my fellow counselors and pastoral professionals to reconsider the use of visualization in therapy. I have learned that the Holy Spirit is the spirit of wisdom and discernment. He is sufficient to help us access subconscious wounds without risking demonic infiltration in the process.

HEALING AND REJECTION

We saw in Chapter 8 that trauma early in life can leave an open doorway for demons. Therefore, an important aspect of inner healing is to explore in detail the potentially harmful rejection present from the womb.

Research suggests that a baby in the womb is sensitive to the emotional climate surrounding it from six months gestation on. Whether a child is wanted or unwanted can profoundly affect the stress the mother feels. A mother who is filled with anger, fear, or other strong emotions will automatically produce stress hormones in her bloodstream, which in turn flood the infant in the womb. Chronic stress during pregnancy is linked to spontaneous abortion. Loud, hateful, angry words spoken during pregnancy can negatively affect the developing baby.

Once the child is born, parental attitudes continue to have a profound effect. If an abortion has been discussed, the ambivalence of the parents toward the child's birth will be communicated, whether the parents intend to express it or not. If they wanted a boy and got a girl, subtle expressions of disappointment come through. These can be the beginnings of rejection and sexual confusion.

I routinely search for signs of early rejection, from conception onward, when taking a case history. What has the client heard about his or her time of conception? Were the parents married? Was he or she wanted? Was the mother sick during pregnancy? It is amazing how much information people absorb from hearing their parents talk.

The Emotion of Healing

At the beginning of an exorcism for a client I'll call Jane, a friend told me that Jane's mother had rejected her when she was pregnant and had tried to abort her. Jane experienced this rejection from her mother throughout her childhood. She grew up believing she was a "bad seed" and lived out this label by becoming a prostitute and being deeply involved in the occult.

The first demons I bound and cast out of Jane were those of rejection and murder. During a break from the session, while we were relaxing and talking, I asked Jane if she had ever had an abortion herself. She became very upset and started to cry. She admitted she'd had an abortion, and she expressed anguish over it.

I asked her to confess the sin to Jesus, which she willingly did. As I was pronouncing absolution with the words "there is more joy in heaven over one sinner who repents," I was suddenly overwhelmed with the palpable presence of the mercy and love of God for Jane. I couldn't finish the absolution. I held her in my arms as we wept together in an overpowering experience of God's mercy and grace. It was about five minutes before either of us could speak. I finally finished the absolution: "There will be more joy in heaven over one sinner who repents than over ninety-nine just persons who need no repentance" (Luke 15:7).

Thawing the Pain

Inner healing is most often a process over time in which layer after layer of pain is brought to the surface for healing. Many people I have worked with have survived the trauma of their lives by burying the pain deep down inside themselves. In a sense, they have placed it in an interior deep freeze, where, they believe, it can safely be ignored.

But life and relationships will not allow us to ignore our pain forever. The unhealed places in our past create emotional handicaps in our present that damage relationships. As people seek help and begin to uncover their past, that frozen pain starts defrosting. And it is pain! Counseling may have been making day-to-day life better for a time, but it is frightening and confusing when pain is suddenly released in a torrent. I often tell clients that once things begin to improve, they should prepare for a release of frozen pain. Because their subconscious minds have now found it is safe enough to acknowledge what was formerly unthinkable, the suppressed memories will surface. Even when they've been prepared, clients often call and say, "You didn't tell me it would hurt this much!"

The same process can release anger, rage, fear, anxiety, and depression. The denial mechanism has been so effective in burying or blocking these emotions that when they are released it is an awesome experience. It is at times like these that I fall back on the healing power of the Holy Spirit. I am grateful it is He, not I, who must do the work.

HEALING THE ANGUISH OF PAST SIN

Every person has done things they are not proud of. One of the most wonderful benefits of being a Christian is the sense of God's forgiveness and the ability to put the past behind forever. But for some the anguished memories of the past almost defy belief. Obtaining God's forgiveness seems an unreachable goal in the eyes of the sinner.

A woman raised in satanism demonstrated to me the awesome power of God's love to forgive and redeem even the most horrifying deeds.

Carla's Story

Raised by two satanist parents, Carla became deeply involved in devil worship. But after years of horror, she came for healing and deliverance.

The most painful part of Carla's healing was the recovery of two horrible memories. The first was that she had given birth to a child who was then sacrificed as an offering to Satan. The second was that she introduced a friend she worked with to satanism. Her friend became a member of a satanic coven, and later, when she was sacrificed, Carla participated in the ceremony.

The awareness of guilt and horror involved in these memories was almost too much for Carla to bear. I was able to lead her through the confession of her sins to Jesus, although because of her emotional state we had to proceed one word at a time. When I pronounced absolution of her sins and forgiveness in the name of Jesus, a powerful demon, named Gatekeeper, put up a last-ditch fight in her. Because of her confession and absolution, he no longer had a legal right to stay, and he left with a loud scream. In the aftermath, I gently laid my hands on Carla in prayer for inner healing. An awesome anointing of the Holy Spirit released a flood of relief, and the peace of God came into her soul. She was filled to overflowing with the love of God.

At a prayer meeting where I was speaking that night, Carla walked in. She was radiant with God's love and looked like a new bride. She was so transformed that many of her friends didn't recognize her.

There is no sin that God cannot forgive and no horror He cannot heal if He is invited to do so. How great is God's love? Ask Carla!

BEYOND EXORCISM

We have seen that inner healing is an integral part of exorcism. It is a process that combines therapeutic intervention with the power of the Holy Spirit. It reaches into the past and the subconscious present. It touches the core of rejection issues that hinders so many of us in our relationships with others and with God. It unleashes powerful emotions, but it does not leave a person to deal with the emotions alone. It destroys the power of unforgiven sin by encouraging repentance and providing forgiveness and absolution. And as sin, trauma, and woundedness are healed, the demonic forces hiding behind them are exposed and can be exorcised.

It is important to note, however, that one does not have to be in need of exorcism to benefit from inner healing. The release of pain and the experience of God's forgiveness and love are joys that every Christian can experience. I pray that the Christian church will hear the cries of the wounded and brokenhearted ever more clearly.

What I have learned is certainly not the last word on inner healing. Many qualified counselors and ministers extend God's love through inner healing with approaches different from mine. I believe the church is just beginning to learn what Jesus wants to teach us about this ministry.

12

THE STORY OF LOU ANN

I am the LORD, the God of all flesh.
Is there anything too hard for Me?
(Jer. 32:27)

I BELIEVE IN miracles. I see God's miracles all the time. One of the most exciting miracles I've ever witnessed was God's total healing of Lou Ann.

This miracle is a marvelous example of the intertwining of inner healing and exorcism, and we can use this case to examine how the principles involved in exorcism are used to actually rid a person of demons. In studying Lou Ann's experience, we can actually see God's hand at work.

I've used a fictitious name for her, but Lou Ann is a real person. The events and experiences I describe here all happened to her. She has given me permission to tell her story in detail, for once she was freed from the many demons manifesting their presence in her life, she committed herself to sharing her witness for Jesus Christ and through Him her victory over Satan.

I met Lou Ann and her husband, John, at a seminar on "Living with Stress Successfully" where I was the speaker. They were there hoping the seminar would give them both some help with a painful condition Lou Ann had suffered for many years that in the previous five years had become intolerable. Her "illnesses" were causing great stress for both of them.

We almost didn't meet, for the seminar sponsor would have cancelled the week's event if he could have reached me. He wanted to tell me that not enough people had pre-registered to cover expenses, but since my wife and I were vacationing, he was unable to call me. He decided to go ahead with the seminar, in spite of the fact he would not be able to pay my full honorarium. He hoped we could work out something. In retrospect, I can see the hand of God involved in arranging for me to meet Lou Ann. She knew she needed help—she'd been searching for help for years—but she didn't know the kind of help she needed. God brought us together and used me in her healing.

I opened the seminar by sharing my faith in Christ. I told the group that we could not talk about stress, particularly the greatest stress a person can face—the death of a loved one—without knowing with certainty that Jesus Christ is the victor over all things of the flesh and, most of all, that He is the victor over death.

At the first break, Lou Ann and John introduced themselves, and she began to tell me of her experience with severe chronic pain. "I have hurt every minute of every day and night for over five years," she said. "I've seen twenty-eight doctors and specialists, had CAT scans, arteriograms, biofeedback, and neuroprobes. I've been fitted with a special TMJ appliance for my mouth, had hours of psychotherapy, and been hospitalized many times. But I still hurt. We're no longer able to get medical insurance, and consequently I've buried John under an overwhelming burden of medical bills. As you can see, we *need* a seminar on stress."

In spite of being an exorcist, initially I had no reason to suspect that Lou Ann's problems were caused by demons. And I am always aware of the danger of suspecting demons are responsible for physical pain or other problems without careful investigation. But Lou Ann said something that made me suspicious.

She said she was surprised and pleased that I had spoken of my Christian faith. She said she liked what I said, but "my pain is worse now than when I walked in here this morning." The suggestion that attending a seminar I was leading could increase her pain was a red flag.

That night during my prayers, I felt God urging me to speak privately with Lou Ann. I began to be burdened that she needed inner healing and exorcism, and I felt led to try to help her.

The next morning she approached me again. This time she said, "Please don't think I am criticizing you. I think what you are saying is wonderful. But my pain is getting worse just being here." Then she asked if we could meet privately. Of course, I agreed.

Later, in private, I asked Lou Ann if she had any explanation for why her pain was worse when she was around me. She said she didn't, but it was clear she knew that being close to me was a factor and had wondered why.

I felt I needed to be very careful of what I would say next. I didn't want to frighten her, but I had to tell her my suspicions. I said, "I hope you won't think I'm crazy, but I believe demonic spirits are involved. They know who I am and they are causing you more pain to make you stay away from me. You see, I am not just a psychologist and pastor, I am also an exorcist, and I am known in the spirit world. Demonic spirits are always afraid of the power God can use against them through someone like me."

She questioned me and wondered how her problems could possibly be traced to demons. She described herself as "a spirit-filled Episcopalian" and a vocalist and choir director in her church. She was active in the Christian Women's Club and was often asked to speak. She was a little skeptical about the existence of demons, but if it were true, it couldn't be true of her. She was a Christian.

"When you sing praise songs, what happens to your pain?" I asked.

"After just one song," she replied, "the pain is so great I have to stop singing."

As gently as I could, I said, "Satan and his fallen angels hate praise music."

I began to question Lou Ann about her history to gather clues of events, circumstances, and choices she had made that might have made doorways through which demons could have entered her life. During our talks over the next several days, I looked for evidence of demon activity.

LOU ANN'S HISTORY

Lou Ann has one sibling, a brother who is two years younger than she. Her mother used guilt to motivate them to try to be perfect. Her father was often absent from the home, either working or fishing, and consequently Lou Ann had a difficult time talking to him. In therapy she came to understand she had always sought a father figure and as an adult had put her husband in the father role. She also transferred that need to her doctors.

She recalled being molested by a farmhand when she was four and that her mother didn't believe her story. She also vaguely remembered a baby-sitter hurting and frightening her, but she couldn't recall the details.

The chronic pain began when Lou Ann's son was beginning first grade. At least once a year for the next several years she was hospitalized for emotional problems. She also had an ulcer and high blood pressure. She began receiving psychotherapy and went from physician to physician, having test after test, trying to learn the causes of her problems. Distraught because of the constant pain and the stress she felt because of it, several times she attempted suicide.

Eventually the diagnosis was temporomandibular joint disorder (TMJ), a condition that causes chronic head, neck, facial, and back pain and usually limited jaw movement. She was fitted with a dental device and told she would never get better. The only foods she could eat were hamburgers, and then only the patty—she could not open her mouth wide enough to take a bite from the bun—and milk shakes. When she was a child, her father would treat her and her younger brother to a trip downtown to the drugstore for a milk shake or a soda when they had been especially good. That memory association made milk shakes very satisfying and comforting. Mostly Lou Ann lived on milk shakes.

Her husband, John, was a good man. He was kind and gentle and very patient with her during all the times she was hospitalized or consulting medical experts about her pain. They had a good sex life until their first child, a daughter, was born. Then Lou Ann lost all interest in sex and would have sexual relations only on their anniversary.

Lou Ann understood herself to be a people pleaser who needed her family's and friends' approval. She was a gifted painter, vocalist, choir director, and public speaker. She described her growing up years as a time of competition with her mother, who was also quite talented. The competition continued into Lou Ann's adult years, at least in Lou Ann's mind, and she had been somewhat estranged from her mother for some time.

Every year, just after Thanksgiving, Lou Ann would lose her voice. The episode always began with a sore throat, but she did not develop an infection or other symptoms of a respiratory problem. One of the psychiatrists she consulted for a time suggested that time of year might be the anniversary of a traumatic event, but because she had suppressed the memory and feelings associated with it, her conscious mind didn't remember. Only her subconscious was disturbed. This is something psychiatrists call "anniversary syndrome."

As her children grew to adulthood, Lou Ann began to suspect that both her son and daughter were homosexual. Eventually, just before Christmas one year, she confronted both of them and they confirmed her suspicions. Each said, "I have felt different since birth." Lou Ann was devastated. She cried uncontrollably and wondered how she could possibly compose herself enough to direct two choirs in the Christmas Eve service.

Lou Ann's greatest fear was that she might lose control in one or more areas of her life. For this reason, she rarely allowed herself to show anger, believing that people shouldn't get angry anyway.

John and Lou Ann went for "primal therapy." She was instructed to let out deep screams while regressing through her memories. But after the therapy, she was worse.

Lou Ann began to work in a Christian counseling center, and she also accelerated her involvements with church work, Christian Women's Club, and other organizations, until she was overloaded with commitments. She realized she was unable to say no. Eventually she was exhausted and feeling so much stress, she wanted an excuse to quit for a while. She thought, "If I had a car accident, then I would have an excuse to slow down." Almost immediately she backed into a utility pole and suffered a severe whiplash. Her head and neck were knocked out of alignment and the additional pain from her injury, coupled with the chronic pain she already suffered, made life unbearable. However, she felt driven to fulfill her commitments. She put on a neck brace and continued on, in spite of intense pain.

She began to dwell on death as an escape from pain. "I became pain," she said. "When I read my diary from the time following the car accident, I find that each day's entry began with, 'Well, the headache is still there' or 'I still have this pain in my stomach' or some other reference to my awareness of pain that would not stop."

On her fiftieth birthday, she told a psychiatrist friend she had a death wish. She said, "I can't go on." Her friend said that if she was looking toward death, she had turned away from God. Lou Ann realized that she had taken her eyes off Jesus.

Lou Ann continued to be regular in her church-related activities and attendance, but during church services she was unable to go to the altar to receive Holy Communion. She spoke with a minister friend about this, wondering why she seemed to be so immovable in church. Very gently he said, "Maybe you don't know Jesus."

As Lou Ann related these events to me, I could see the evidence of demons at work. The circumstances surrounding her car accident, for example, seemed highly suggestive of demonic presence, but there were two other episodes that were particularly convincing.

One occurred when she was making the hundred-mile trip to the dentist who was treating her for her TMJ condition. On this particular occasion, during the drive the car went off the road three times. Feeling absolutely powerless to control the car, Lou Ann was convinced "something" was trying to kill her. The other event, however, is even more indicative of the presence of demonic spirits surrounding and controlling Lou Ann.

During one of her many attempts to receive help through psychiatry, a psychiatrist from whom she'd received therapy for a number of years, suggested they try a sodium pentathol interview to attempt to find out what was blocking Lou Ann's progress. She agreed, provided the session was tape recorded so that she could be aware later of what went on.

Usually half a vial of pentathol is all that is necessary to put a person "under," but Lou Ann was so unresponsive and so in control, the doctor had to administer three vials before he could begin the interview. After this high dosage of sodium pentathol, he was able to get her to respond, but when he approached a sensitive subject, suddenly a voice coming from Lou Ann said, "Stop! Don't tell him any more!"

The doctor asked, "Who said that?" but there was no answer.

"Did your mother say that?" he asked.

"No," the voice replied.

"Did your father say that?"

"No."

"*Who* said that?" the doctor asked again.

Then an awful-sounding, loud voice announced, "Lou Ann says that!"

I was convinced. I informed Lou Ann, "That was a demon speaking through you."

Even though the idea that demonic spirits could be controlling her seemed bizarre, this explanation made sense to Lou Ann. And when I invited her to come to Phoenix for a week or two of intensive inner healing and deliverance, she indicated interest if the arrangements could be made.

Looking back, I find it hard to believe that I was so bold and brazen as to believe Lou Ann could be healed and set free in one or two weeks, considering that twenty-eight medical specialists had told her she would never be healed. One specialist had even said that she would never sing again. In his opinion there were only three specialists in the country who might be able to help her. But, due to the overwhelming debt Lou Ann and John had already amassed trying to find solutions to her misery and the fact that they no longer could get medical insurance to pay for her care, seeing additional doctors was out of the question.

The only way I can explain my confidence that God would heal Lou Ann in one or two weeks is that He has given me the gift of blind faith. Because I believed my meeting Lou Ann was a divinely set appointment, I also believed God was in charge of what would happen in Phoenix. My part was to obey Him and pray for guidance for myself and healing for Lou Ann. Just the same, I knew Lou Ann's healing would involve intense struggle. In other words, it would be a battle royal.

I prayed for Lou Ann before she left me, asking God to begin healing her right then. The anointing was so strong that Lou Ann left "drunk" in the Holy Spirit. That powerful anointing was a dear sign to me that God wanted Lou Ann to come to Phoenix to be healed. And it reminded me again of God's words in Jeremiah 32:27, "Behold, I am the LORD, the God of all flesh. Is there anything too hard for Me?"

In the weeks ahead God's hand was evident as we moved toward the time of exorcism, making arrangements for Lou Ann to spend time in Phoenix and preparing ourselves for a mighty battle with demonic forces, while the spirits tried to prevent Lou Ann's being set free.

PREPARING FOR EXORCISM

Lou Ann and John returned to their home and began to pray about a trip to Phoenix. Shortly after, she sent me a letter. In part she said:

> I have not known how I could afford going to see you, so I made that part of my prayer. (My poor hubby has been spent into the poorhouse trying to pay my medical bills these past five years.) Then through some amazing *God-incidences* (there just aren't any coincidences any more), a friend has offered to pay my way. But how can I take advantage of her? I could never repay her.
>
> At this point, I don't know what I'll do. To be truthful, I'm afraid of the pain—both emotional and physical—that I just know would accompany our time together. I know the Lord doesn't give us a spirit of fear, but I also know Satan doesn't want me to come and see you.

Eventually Lou Ann decided to accept her friend's offer. The decision was also made for the friend, Mary, to accompany Lou Ann to Phoenix.

They arrived on the last Sunday in October. I had asked them to bring any diaries or other records that would shed light on important crisis times in Lou Ann's life, particularly when she was growing up. I still had few clues to the tacit agreements she had made with Satan or other events that might have made doorways Satan's evil spirits could use to enter her life. I still didn't know exactly what I was dealing with—just that the demonic spirits were powerful.

When I met Mary, I was aware of her deep love for Jesus. It radiated from her face and shone from her eyes. I asked if she would help with the exorcism, and she replied, "I've never assisted in an exorcism, but I'm afraid not to help." I soon learned that Mary is a powerful intercessor. The hand of God was at work in bringing Mary to Phoenix to participate in Lou Ann's exorcism.

From the airport we went immediately to my office. I gave Lou Ann a tablet and asked her to write *Jesus sets me free*. Her normal handwriting is so small and compact, I asked her to write it again larger, and again until she had written *Jesus sets me free* in large, bold letters. Then we began to review her diaries, and she showed me a list of points she had extracted from the one she kept during the year following her car accident. Some of the points were quite revealing. All showed significant pain and despair.

I spent most of my time in bed, either crying or doped up on Demerol. I went to the hospital many times for pain medication.

I couldn't wear makeup because the slightest wisp of a touch caused me severe pain.

My left arm was numb most of the time and I dropped things suddenly, unable to hold them in my hand.

I was dizzy and nauseated, needing to hold on to the walls most of the time.

I couldn't drive.

I had a tennis-ball-sized lump on my shoulder that just became a part of me.

I had diarrhea almost constantly.

I couldn't wear earrings and could stand only the slightest, tiniest necklaces. I had to give up the gold necklace that I'd never taken off since John gave it to me.

I wore a collar brace for months because my neck was so weak it wouldn't hold up my head.

I had a very unsettling fear of crowds, even though I'd always loved the excitement of being a part of large groups. At our church coffee hours, I stood way over in a corner so that no one could jostle me or approach me from behind. Shopping was just out. Hugs were totally and depressingly out of the picture. I couldn't even reach up in the slightest way to kiss my husband or have him kiss me.

I couldn't hold a book. Even the newspaper was too big to hold. Singing in church was impossible—I couldn't hold the hymnal to see the words.

When I sang, my throat hurt.

After two hospital stays and many EKGs, I knew the chest pains were all in my head.

We went to the mountains twice in a year and a half, but I wished I had stayed at home. The air pressure changes going up and coming down caused me such severe pain, I had to take Demerol.

Once a month, and with every stressful event, as well, I had an ugly, painful cold sore.

Lifting even one hair on my head hurt so much I cried. I was extremely depressed and twice made plans to kill myself.

Lou Ann also had kept a journal she called "TMJ—The Agony and the Ecstasy." In it she had written a few quotations of what others had said about pain and her own feelings as well.

Pain has scraped away the last visible traces of hope off the edges of my soul.
                                         —Joyce Landorf

Pain is a language without words, and so it is untouched by words.
                                         —Susan Lenekes

My pain. I've had headaches and phantom toothaches for years, but increasingly the pain has become a bigger part of my life; in fact, it has taken over my life.

You are not healed because:
   A. You do not have enough faith.
   B. You obviously have sin in your life.
   C. Your pain is purely psychosomatic.
   D. All of the above.

Read Job if you think you are suffering.

Nobody said life would be easy.

Sometimes Christians hurt me more than my pain.

I'm so tired
I want to drive my car off a cliff
and not hurt any more.

But
what do I do with
"Thou shalt not murder"?
Being a Christian sure reduces my alternatives.

I can't see God any more—Help!
I need a rest.
I'm so tired of staying "up."
I don't want to fight any more.
I don't want to die either.
I just want the pain to stop.

So many hurting—so few comforting.

It's not fair!
I'm so discouraged.
The knives are back—
Stabbing red hot into my back and neck.
The sledge hammer of excruciating pain has hit my jaw.
My left cheek is swollen beyond belief (except I look fine).
It just doesn't seem fair sometimes.
I've tried so hard to do everything
and to do nothing.
And I'm forced once more to lie
and do nothing while my mind
tries to keep from screaming.

After reading these descriptions of her life of pain, I said,
"Lou Ann, do you want to be healed?"

My question caught her off guard and for a moment she
was quiet. Then she said, "Of course."

I explained she would have to want to be healed and she
would have to fight for her healing. The chronic-pain person, just as anyone who is chronically ill, often quietly surrenders to hopelessness and depression, becoming very
passive and doubting that healing is possible. He or she
will often have the attitude, "If there can be healing, well,
you go ahead and heal me (but I doubt that you can)."

Then I asked, "Do you believe you can be healed? Can you see yourself healed and without pain? Do you believe God can heal you?" At that time Lou Ann could say the words, "I believe I can be healed," but she could not express them as a statement of faith in God's power to heal her. Like so many others, her pain and illness had become who she was. She could not perceive herself any other way. And she had developed a powerful psychological mechanism of denial in order to survive the chronic pain. She had survived by controlling her emotions totally. To be healed she would have to surrender her control to God and tear down thick walls of denial. It would not be easy.

THE EXORCISM

Monday, The First Day

We drove to the beautiful little chapel of the church where I was a member. As we approached the door, Lou Ann stopped. She was immobilized, unable to walk further toward the building. I took her by the arm and led her into the chapel.

Inside was a beautiful altar with a kneeler in front of it. The sound system allowed us to play praise music. The chapel was deserted except for us.

I put a praise music tape on the player and we received the sacrament of the Lord's Supper. I anointed Lou Ann with oil and, laying my hands on her head, said, "I take authority in the name of Jesus, and I break every curse from every doctor, nurse, or any other person who has told Lou Ann that there is no hope for her, that she will have to live in pain for the rest of her life. I break the curse of every one of those words from her conscious mind, her subconscious mind, her memory, her emotions, her will, and her body, and I break the effect of those words from every area of her being. I cover each word with the blood of Jesus and rebuke every demon assigned to those words."

The words of authority figures exert great power and effect on the person who trusts and hears the words, especially if the messages are stated repetitively. Twenty-eight medical specialists had told Lou Ann there was no hope for healing her chronic pain, and she had looked up to her doctors as though they were "gods" and believed what they said was "truth."

She was in Phoenix, in a chapel with Mary and me, filled with unbelief, wondering why she was there and if demons could be real. "There is hope, Lou Ann," I said. "Our Lord Jesus heals the brokenhearted and sets the captives free."

I spent most of the first day in laying on of hands for inner healing of her memories and damaged emotions and reading from the eleventh chapter of Hebrews. We talked about faith as a spiritual gift. "Now faith is the substance of things hoped for, the evidence of things not seen [or felt]" (Heb. 11:1), I reminded her, and pointed out that she had been a victim so long she had asked the spirit of passivity to put her will in bondage. Pain and the demonic had programmed her to accept being hopeless and victimized. As the day wore on and there was no demonic manifestation, she became discouraged. That night she had a vision.

I was standing below two huge, thick wooden doors. It seemed like the scene you have when you look up at a big skyscraper. There were large brass rings and I was too small to reach them but, as I stopped there, I reached out and just barely touched the doors. They gently, silently drifted open. I stepped through and into a blue sky that stretched as far as I could see.

I have never felt such a sense of eternity. I was afraid, though, because I was just standing there staring into a vast space. But it was a warm, wonderful space.

Then I made a wonderful discovery. As I took a step, there, under my foot, a stone appeared. With each hesitant new step, there was another stone solid beneath my foot.

But the best thing of all was that, when I looked back, all

the stones behind me had turned to gold and were en-
crusted with all kinds of precious stones glittering in a blaz-
ing sunlight!

This wonderful vision from God was not all that happened that night. There was a war going on inside Lou
Ann. Later, after the vision, she began to shake. She tossed
around in her bed like a rag doll. The next morning when I
arrived to drive her and Mary to the chapel, Lou Ann didn't
want to go. She was afraid of what Satan might do. Finally
she admitted that she believed Satan had more power than
God. That morning and many times in the days ahead, I
said, "Remember the vision, Lou Ann. Reach out! Take one
more step."

Tuesday, The Second Day

On the second day, as we walked toward the chapel
door, again something stopped Lou Ann and she was unable to move forward. Mary and I had to physically lead her
inside the building. Once inside, I had a strong sense that
the demonic spirits were agitated. I put a crucifix in Lou
Ann's hands, and it felt like fire to her. I put the crucifix on
her forehead, and again it was very hot.

I asked her to kneel before the Lord at the altar and ask
forgiveness for her doubts that persisted even after the vision of her faith walk and to break every tacit agreement
with the spirit of doubt. Then I bound the spirit of doubt
and commanded it to leave. Lou Ann began to cough and
spit out phlegm. She was very aware of the demon leaving
her.

I believed that with all the pain Lou Ann had endured,
demonic spirits must be hooked into her emotional pain,
her painful memories, and her physical pain. I commanded
the spirit of pain to leave her, but it was a powerful strong
man and would not leave.

There was also a strong man of death and under his dominion was the spirit of suicide. Lou Ann knelt again at the alter and confessed her sin of suicidal thoughts and attempts. She broke every tacit agreement with the spirit of suicide and pronounced the absolution of her sins, and confessed and declared the tacit agreements with the spirit of suicide broken, cut off from her, and cast down. In time the spirit of suicide left her.

I was concerned that Lou Ann was not merely passive about her inner healing and exorcism, but that she was fighting against Mary and me. I knew the spirit of death would not leave unless she began to fight him; therefore, we took some time to talk about her resistance.

She quickly assured me that she was not an angry person, neither filled with rage, nor rebellious. But I pointed out that she rebelled often, even when I asked her to lift her arms toward God during praise music. She really was not taking authority over the demons.

Lou Ann made some mocking comments about God's lack of power and I bound off the spirit of mockery and commanded it to leave. I continued to pray and read aloud 1 Samuel 15:22–23: "Has the Lord as much pleasure in your burnt offerings and sacrifices as in your obedience? Obedience is far better than sacrifice. He is much more interested in your listening to him than in your offering the fat of rams to him. For rebellion is as bad as the sin of witchcraft, and stubbornness is as bad as worshiping idols" (TLB).

This was an exhausting day and Lou Ann was surprised at how powerful the demon of rebellion was because she had always been a people pleaser and a perfectionist. This demon was tenacious; nevertheless, it left her.

That night as I prayed for guidance and insight, I realized that very powerful demonic spirits had attached themselves to Lou Ann. Possibly these spirits were passed down to her from her ancestors, but it seemed more likely they were connected to some early emotional trauma that had not been healed.

When the demonic attaches to a young child, it seems to wrap itself around the child's personality. The child never knows himself or herself to be different from the tormented individual that results. He thinks, "That's just the way I am." This is why the Holy Spirit's inner healing is so necessary in separating the individual from the demonic. And this is why, during periods of quiet between periods of demonic manifestation, I lay hands on the person for the Holy Spirit to do His healing work.

Wednesday, The Third Day

I was determined that Wednesday would be a battle royal, even if we had to work all day and come back after supper. Time was passing and Lou Ann was exhausted and depressed. She had verbalized her doubts and said she felt the enemy was winning. I talked to her about her disappointment in God's not healing her of all her pain after all the years she had sought help.

"Did you ever get angry at God?" I asked.

"No, I don't think so," she said. "But it's not fair. I love Jesus. I used to serve the Lord with the gift of song and I directed church choirs. I am a witness in sharing my faith at Christian Women's Clubs, but I don't have much to share of God's Good News."

"Do you feel that God has let you down?"

"I just think it's disgusting that you want me to throw up in this 'demon bucket'! Can't God deal with me in a more civilized manner? Maybe He doesn't hear my prayers."

"Have you felt it isn't fair that your son and daughter are both homosexual?"

Lou Ann began to talk about how much she loved her two children and how gifted they were. She took out a cassette tape of Barbra Streisand and said, "I think God wants me to play this. It's 'A Child is Born.' It's the thoughts and dreams of a mother as she holds her infant daughter in her arms."

She played the song over and over many times. Slowly

the music defrosted the pain Lou Ann felt because of the homosexuality of her children and the agony she had not allowed herself to express. She cried and cried, and out of the pit of pain came anger and blasphemy. I bound off the spirit of blasphemy from her damaged emotions and memories and in the name of Jesus commanded it to leave.

Grieving over her children made Lou Ann realize the hopelessness she felt of her children ever being normal. Hopelessness was a powerful spirit controlling all areas of her life. Hadn't twenty-eight medical specialists said she was hopeless? She believed her situation was hopeless and this hopelessness had led her to suicidal thoughts and attempts to kill herself. She broke the tacit agreement with the spirit of hopelessness and renounced hopelessness and despair.

"I waited patiently for God to help me," I read from Psalms. "Then he listened and heard my cry. He lifted me out of the pit of despair, out from the bog and the mire, and set my feet on a hard, firm path and steadied me as I walked along. He has given me a new song to sing, of praises to our God" (40:1–3, TLB).

I put a praise tape in the player and asked Lou Ann and Mary to sing with me. Mary joined in immediately, and we sang for about fifteen minutes, but Lou Ann hesitated. Eventually she began to sing, hesitantly at first because of the pain singing caused her. By the time we were finished, she was singing lustily and lifting her arms toward heaven without assistance.

"I bind off the spirit of hopelessness and in Jesus' name I command it to leave you!"

Thursday, The Fourth Day

Lou Ann was depressed and exhausted. She wanted to quit and go home. I decided we needed a day off. Both Mary and Lou Ann needed to relax and Lou Ann had a lot of powerful emotions concerning her children to process and bring to the surface to be healed.

Friday, The Fifth Day

I told Lou Ann we would need more than one week and asked her and Mary to agree to stay. Lou Ann said, "Another week? I don't know if I can take it."

"You can't quit now."

"Don't you ever give up and quit, Ken?"

"No. When God gives me a job to do, He never tells me how long it will take. I just stay with it until it's finished. We are at a crucial time in your healing. Satan wants you to quit because he doesn't want a healed Lou Ann going about singing praises to God and telling the world how God healed you and set you free. You can quit and stay in pain and bondage to Satan, or you can work out your healing as the ten lepers did."

So often in an exorcism the crisis of choice is present— the choice between Satan and Christ, life and death, curse or blessing. I read aloud Deuteronomy 30:15-19.

> Look, today I have set before you life and death, depending on whether you obey or disobey. I have commanded you today to love the Lord your God and to follow His paths and to keep His laws, so that you will live and become a great nation, and so that the Lord your God will bless you and the land you are about to possess. But if your hearts turn away and you won't listen—if you are drawn away to worship other gods—then I declare to you this day that you shall surely perish; you will not have a long, good life in the land you are going in to possess.
>
> I call heaven and earth to witness against you that today I have set before you life or death, blessing or curse. Oh, that you would choose life; that you and your children might live! (TLB)

This was a real turning point for Lou Ann. She had to decide to go on with God, obeying Him and following His guidance, and facing the emotional, mental, and physical pain healing would cause her plus the fury of Satan, or she could give in to Satan. Lou Ann squirmed uncomfortably at the choice she must make.

"I called the woman whom God has assigned as an intercessor for me," I said, "and asked her to ask the Lord for His guidance. We are at a crucial crossroad, not only in your exorcism, but in your life on earth and for eternity. I gave her no information about you, saying only that we are in a powerful war with Satan. This is what she heard this morning:

> If you continue to deny your weakness after seeing what I have done for you, then I will deny you before my Father.
>
> I have a unique ministry for you. I called you from the foundation of the world. I have wooed you. I have led you. I have my hand on you. Yield to the ministry of my servant and follow what I have given him and you will be set totally free. Deny his ministry and you deny me. You will go home worse than when you came.
>
> I gave you a free will and a free choice. Choose the good and you will have eternal life. Choose evil and you will not have the wonderful things I have planned for you.
>
> This is your choice!"

The demonic spirits were doing their best to prevent Lou Ann's choosing life. Satan had lied to her, telling her, "If you say yes to Jesus, you will end up being persecuted and killed on a cross like He was." It's called "let's make a deal." It is Satan's way of trying to make you stay where you are, where you think you know how to survive. He makes you think that if you follow Jesus, you will endure greater pain and suffering and even death. He tries to convince you that staying with him is the better deal.

I challenged Lou Ann about these lies of Satan's. I said, "Satan has been trying to kill you, so going on with Jesus, even to the Cross, is still better than the hell you are in right now. Yes, you will experience physical and emotional pain before you are set free, but Jesus will set you free. Satan will keep you in bondage forever."

The grip of the powerful spirit of death began to manifest itself by taking control of Lou Ann's hands and putting them around her neck, trying to choke her to death. It took all the strength I had to pull her hands off her throat. Then we sang praise music, one song after another, and filled that little chapel with music. And we felt the real and powerful presence of the Holy Spirit.

The demon of masochism had lied to Lou Ann, trying to convince her that her role in life was to suffer this pain. She had made a tacit agreement that in some way seemed to make sense to her. The agreement was based partially on the teaching of "redemptive suffering," which means that the sickness and pain a person suffers is to be given to God for Him to use as a blessing to others. But a person living with chronic pain seldom feels blessed or feels like praising God for the pain and sickness. Still this teaching is a powerful block for a suffering person to overcome.

This teaching fails to recognize that Jesus came to heal the sick and set the captives free. He did not come to give us sickness and pain so God could be glorified. The suffering we face as Christians is because of faith and obedience to Jesus Christ. That suffering is not sickness and pain, but persecution for one's faith. Lou Ann had to break a tacit agreement with the spirit of masochism, renounce it, and cast it down before it would leave.

Another suicide attempt surfaced in her memory. The Lord healed the memories and the demon left. Tied into the spirit of suicide were tormenting spirits who magnified her pain and tormented her thoughts, trying to influence her to choose death by suicide as a way out of the tormenting pain. Lou Ann renounced them and they left.

The Holy Spirit led us to pray about rejection and the fear of rejection. The wounds of rejection and fear of rejection are the forces that drive a person who wants approval in order to feel accepted to become a perfectionist. In her attempt to be perfect, Lou Ann felt secure so long as she had control over her emotions, the people around her, and the circumstances of her life. This controlling mechanism provided a degree of emotional security.

She had received the spirit of control from her mother and this spirit fought mightily against her decision to let God be in control of her life. Letting go, especially of her will, was frightening. I think that is why God gave her that beautiful vision of a faith walk and showed her that as she took each step, He would put up a step stone to hold her.

I have found this step of faith—giving total control over my life to God the Father—the most difficult act of surrender I've had to make. I believe that is why He gave me the gift of *blind* faith so I could trust in Him and walk in simple obedience.

Lou Ann chose life and we spent a beautiful time singing praises to God. We ended the thirteen-hour day on our knees, thanking God for His goodness, and I went to sleep certain the spiritual high would carry over to the next morning when we would be victorious.

Saturday, The Sixth Day

The sixth day was Halloween and the spiritual high from the previous evening did not last. Lou Ann was stubborn and rebellious. She fought me about staying in the chapel. Several times she tried to strike and choke me, but her hands were stopped by an invisible shield around me. At times like that, Scripture is especially meaningful as well as comforting. I remembered and quoted, "For he orders his angels to protect you wherever you go" (Ps. 91:11, TLB) and " 'Touch not these chosen ones of mine,' he warned, 'and do not hurt my prophets' " (Ps. 105:15, TLB).

The Lord intervened and told Lou Ann to prostrate herself before the altar. The Holy Spirit revealed she had made a tacit agreement to keep the pain as an escape from the demands of her job. She renounced her pact with Satan and confessed her sins of narcissism and bitterness. The Lord gave her absolution and these demons left her.

It was time for Lou Ann to intercede for the sins of her family. We talked about the broken relationships in her family and how proud and unforgiving some of her relatives were. She made a list of the sins of her family and the bondages she wanted broken and placed this list on the altar.

I read in Exodus 32:7-14 of Moses interceding for the sins of Israel after they built the golden calf. God was angry and determined He would destroy His rebellious and stubborn people, but Moses begged God to "turn back" from His "fierce wrath," and "so the Lord changed his mind and spared them" (v. 12–14, TLB). I also read Nehemiah 9:1–3, which describes the people of Israel taking turns to confess their own sins and those of their ancestors.

As Lou Ann knelt before the altar, she called each of her relatives by name and read their sins from the list she'd made. She asked God to forgive them and to forgive any sins she hadn't remembered and any relative she hadn't named. Again the presence of the Holy Spirit was powerfully evident, and Lou Ann received the sacraments, repeating after me, "This is the new covenant given in the blood of Jesus for the forgiveness of our sins and the sins of others."

Sunday, The Seventh Day

Early in the morning, Lou Ann called her parents. Her mother was at home alone; her father had gone fishing. The mother said something had happened inside her the day before. She didn't know what happened, but she felt different. Lou Ann had a sense of acceptance by her mother that she had not known before. As the conversation closed, her mother said, "I love you."

This day, as with all days concerned with exorcism, time

had no meaning, for earthly time is not the same as super-natural time. And as on the previous days, I spent time in laying on of hands for the Holy Spirit to reveal what needed to be revealed and healed. At first the memories came in bits and pieces, but this day the event surfaced clearly and in full detail. It was the beginning of a major breakthrough and revealed a woundedness that opened the doorway for powerful demons to enter Lou Ann's life.

"I was four years old and my brother was two. Usually if my mom and dad went out, we stayed with the nice couple next door, but this time they had a high school girl stay with us for a whole weekend. She let us blow big bubbles with bubble gum. That was fun until she made us blow bigger and bigger bubbles that popped and stuck all over our faces. And she wouldn't let us take the gum off until it had hardened. Then she pulled it off, pulling out our eye-brows and hair. And when we cried, she laughed.

"Then she asked what food we hated most. We both said, 'cottage cheese!' She gave each of us a whole carton of cottage cheese and made us sit beside the floor furnace. She said we had to eat all the cottage cheese or she would hold us over the furnace until we burned up. My little brother didn't want to eat his cottage cheese—he didn't like it at all. She removed the grate from the furnace and held him over the flame, moving him closer and closer to it. I was terrified. In time he stopped crying and promised to eat the cottage cheese. It seemed like we sat there for hours.

"Next she took us in a closet. As we sat on the floor in the pitch black, she scratched and knocked on the walls and floor, saying, 'Do you hear that? It's Yahootie and he's going to *get you!*'

"While we sat there waiting for Yahootie to come back, she touched me. I was confused by the terror and the little quivers I felt.

"Then she took my little brother out of the closet and told me not to move—*no matter what!* I was too afraid to move, so I waited. I heard evil sounding laughter, but I didn't hear any sounds of my brother. I was very worried about him, so after a while I opened the door and peeped out.

"The girl was sitting on top of the carpet that was all rolled up, but I didn't see my brother anywhere. Then I knew he was inside the carpet.

"I ran away from her—down the stairs and over to the people next door. I told them and they followed me back but they were old and couldn't run as fast as I could. The baby-sitter was furious with me. Never again since then have I seen such rage. She yelled, 'You little snitch! I'll kill you for that!' She was trying to choke me when the neighbors came into the room. By the time they got my little brother out of the rug, he was blue from suffocation, but they were able to revive him.

"After that my brother and I were certain Yahootie was upstairs in our room and would get us while we were sleeping. So every night after our parents tucked us in bed, I sneaked into my brother's room and we pretended to make chocolate sodas. We went through all the motions and when we were finished, we told Yahootie that he could have our sodas if he would leave us alone that night."

Two frightened, wounded children, trying to keep themselves safe, innocently made a pact with Satan, and the power demon of death entered Lou Ann's life. These events were so traumatic, she suppressed the memories, but the demon was there in her life tormenting and controlling her. And this demon didn't intend to leave her.

She began to experience the cold of death, and her temperature dropped until her body was ice cold to my touch and the spirit presence was very evident in the chapel. The demon caused Lou Ann to pace through the chapel and to bang her head on the walls. I had to wrestle her to the floor to prevent an injury. She lay down between two pews and screamed and pounded the floor.

Finally there was a release of rage and phlegm. Lou Ann was very frightened by the powerful presence of death and the release of the demon of rage. "Please don't let Satan get me," she pled with me, over and over. "There are chants echoing inside my head. Why won't the spirit of death leave me? I know he is very agitated, and he won't let me drink the holy water. I've experienced a spiritual realm I never believed existed. It's terrifying!"

That night, back in her motel room, Lou Ann got into a tub of hot water hoping to get warm and stayed until 2:00 A.M. Later God gave Lou Ann a second vision.

She was lying huddled in her bed and Jesus entered the room. He picked her up and, holding her in His arms, walked toward the closet where the baby-sitter had put her when she was four years old. She thought He would open the door and turn on the light inside. But, instead, He kicked out the wall and knocked the closet completely out of the house. When He was finished, He had demolished that side of the house.

Monday, The Eighth Day

Unfortunately I had a personal requirement to attend to and had to leave Lou Ann and Mary on their own for most of the day. This event was important in my professional life, but I was concerned about Lou Ann. We were in a very sensitive period with her healing. I tried to speed things along in order to get back to her quickly, but I wasn't free until late afternoon, and I couldn't meet Lou Ann and Mary until dinnertime. But at dinner Lou Ann recalled a time years before when she had gone into a rage very much like the one we had witnessed the day before in the chapel.

She was hospitalized for dangerously high blood pressure. She became frantic and began to pace. "Finally I went to the room where they kept the clean linen. I began screaming and pulling sheets, gowns, towels, and so forth, off the shelves, until two nurses forced me into a cold shower and a third nurse gave me a shot of something.

"I still can't believe I did that. The rage just erupted, but it wasn't me. And I never did it again until last night."

Even though I was very tired after a traumatic day and Mary and Lou Ann both thought I should go home, I wanted the three of us to go to the chapel—at least for a while. I felt we needed to pray and have communion.

Lou Ann tried to play the piano, but gave up, saying, "I can't seem to get my fingers and my mind to coordinate. It's so strange." Then she said, "I realize I have a fear of love—even God's love."

Immediately there was a great outpouring of the Holy Spirit. The chapel was aglow with the presence of God, and He spoke to Lou Ann: "I know your pain. You can be a powerful witness because all the powerful ones have suffered." Lou Ann could not feel God's love, but Mary and I were being filled with His love and power. It was awesome to be present at such a powerful anointing of the Holy Spirit.

Following the anointing, demons of doubt, fear of love, homosexuality, incest, and mockery left Lou Ann. But the demon of death held her left side and manifested itself by making her arm and hand move in strange motions and then getting very cold and going numb. Still the demon of death would not leave.

I felt there was either something I was missing or something she had not revealed that gave this power demon of death the legal right to remain.

Tuesday, The Ninth Day

The next morning when I met Lou Ann and Mary to go to the chapel, Lou Ann said, "I sensed you were in the parking lot before you came inside. It was the same feeling

I had the first time we met. I didn't know you, but something inside me knew you. I feel the same way when you reach for a cup of holy water. Remember last night you reached for the holy water and the demon said, 'I've been here before?'

Wednesday, The Tenth Day

The demons manifested themselves more quickly and left without much struggle. That was one of the strange things about Lou Ann's exorcism. The demons took a long time to manifest themselves, longer than with any other exorcism I had experienced. But once they did, they usually left quickly. However, the strong man demons would not release their hold.

Thursday, The Eleventh Day

We started at the chapel at 8:30 A.M. The spirit of voodoo manifested and left with an ear-piercing scream. This demon must have come from the demonized baby-sitter. The power demon of death tried to choke Lou Ann, and she couldn't get her breath. I placed my hand on the area of the choking and the Holy Spirit broke the choke. Even Mary was afraid, fearing that she and Lou Ann both would die. I poured holy water into their mouths.

That evening we couldn't use the chapel and went instead to my office. But because some people were working next door, we felt my office wasn't comfortable. As we walked toward my car, suddenly I realized Lou Ann wasn't with us. She was hanging on to the stair railing and shaking violently. I managed to grab her before the demon could force her to fall. She was very cold and very frightened. Once we got her in the car, a demon growled and said, "If I can't have her, you can't either." I knew it was urgent that we cast out these demons. Right there in my car, I commanded them to leave her, and they did. Lou Ann felt a great release and then an exhausted peace. She said, "I sensed it crying all the way back to the pit."

Friday, The Twelfth Day

We were back at the chapel, singing praise music, when several women of the church came to get some boxes of homemade items left there for a rummage sale. A beautiful rag doll fell from one of the boxes. Lou Ann bought it and named it Lulu. I told Lou Ann that Lulu was a symbol of her being set free and that she had permission to feel all the emotions of childhood and to become as a little child with Abba Father.

As she held the doll, I began a very painful part of her exorcism. I touched each of the trigger points of muscle spasm pain and said, "If by the finger of God I cast out demons, then you know the Kingdom of God is here." At each touch a demon left that trigger point. Lou Ann's physical pain was excruciating. I use trigger point therapy, or "myotherapy," for releasing muscle spasm pain in people who have chronic stress because of muscle spasms, such as the TMJ pain Lou Ann suffered.

Several times Lou Ann wanted to quit, but I encouraged her, saying, "You can't quit! You can face walking through this pain to have the final victory over all these demons of pain."

When I finished the trigger point cleansing of demons, Lou Ann's bottom jaw had realigned one full tooth, and her dental appliance no longer fit her mouth. She was filled with joy and, as the Holy Spirit anointed her, she said, "Now I know God's peace that is not like anything of this world. Finally I have experienced God's love—so warm, so gentle, so all encompassing. It is so beautiful. You said, 'I bind you, spirit of resignation from life, resignation to pain, and resignation to death, and I cast you out in the name of Jesus Christ,' and the spirits of resignation and death left me.

"Praise God! My weak, lifeless arms are suddenly being lifted up. The pain is gone! In the name of Jesus, Satan had to flee, because in the name of Jesus I am free!"

AFTER THE EXORCISM

Lou Ann returned to her home and experienced a loving, exciting reunion with her husband. They both rejoiced at the change in their sex life.

And her relationship with her mother and father was different also. The intercessory prayer she had offered for them on Halloween had changed them both as well as other members of their family. Two of Lou Ann's uncles, both in their mid-fifties, had been estranged for many years. Their bitterness was so great, they would not speak to each other or be in any place together. Even when their mother lay dying, neither would visit her if the other might be there. But on the day Lou Ann prayed for forgiveness of the sins of all her relatives and asked God to set them free from bondage, one brother began to have the desire to visit the other and make amends.

Once again Lou Ann could sing, and she dedicated herself to sharing her witness of Jesus Christ and His victory over Satan. But Satan wasn't finished with her.

Several months after her exorcism, her doctors discovered a cancer in her breast. She called me to ask that I pray for her during the surgery, and God revealed to me that this disease was the result of a curse. I said, "I have to break the curse of death from witchcraft from you," and over the phone I broke the curse and commanded the demon of death to leave her.

She said, "Oh! I just felt something lift off my head!"

She asked the priest and the congregation of her church to pray for her. The priest laid his hand on her while the people prayed for the Holy Spirit to intervene, and Lou Ann felt a surge of the Holy Spirit's power.

The surgery a few days later revealed that all the cancerous lymph nodes were strangely burned from the inside out. The cancer was gone.

I praise God for His healing. He restored Lou Ann to vibrant life and enabled her to be victorious. And He claimed Mary for Himself as well. She now serves Him full-time in a ministry of inner healing and exorcism.

What a wonderful God we serve!

13

HEALING RITUAL ABUSE SURVIVORS

Behold, I give you the authority to
trample on serpents and scorpions, and
over all the power of the enemy, and
nothing shall by any means hurt you.

(Luke 10:19)

HEALING AND EXORCISM for survivors of satanic ritual
abuse are the most challenging and difficult forms of deliverance. Satan worshipers attack defenseless, vulnerable
children, robbing them of normal development and
healthy personalities and inflicting life-long emotional
damage. Without the powerful intervention of the Holy
Spirit, these victims have no hope of recovery.

Satanic ritual abuse (SRA) is just emerging as a focus of
clinical psychology, and therapists and counselors who are
equipped to deal with SRA survivors are still scarce. Those
psychologists who do treat SRA survivors often completely
ignore the spiritual dimension of the abuse. For this reason,
parents who discover their child has been the victim of
SRA may have to provide deliverance and healing to the
child themselves.

SYMPTOMS OF RITUAL ABUSE

A child can be exploited by a satanist in many different settings: preschool, grade school, in a community organization, at a friend's house, at camp, even at a church youth group. Certainly most organizations and activities provide safe and healthy experiences for children, but satanists have infiltrated all kinds of groups, and parents must be vigilant. Be suspicious if you notice any of the following symptoms.

Personality changes. Noticeable or sudden changes in personality can be a signal of abuse. For instance, if a loving, easygoing child suddenly becomes aggressive, violent, or sexually demonstrative, or if a confident child becomes fearful, plagued with nightmares or night terrors, that is a warning sign.

Unreasonable fear. Exaggerated fear can be expressed in many ways. An abnormal fear of being left with a baby-sitter, emotional regression to a younger age, clinging to Mother, fear of going to the bathroom, fear of eating certain things, fear of parents dying, a serious preoccupation with death or talking of coffins, dead people, or dead animals can be important indicators of SRA.

Children can develop an unreasonable fear of police officers, clergy, doctors, judges, or religious objects such as a crucifix or a particular picture of Jesus. Even cartoon characters might suddenly become frightening. Fear of small places or of being put in a box, a sudden fear of water or of being kidnapped, or a fear of colors such as black, red, or purple should cause suspicion.

Sometimes the fear is expressed as pain in the stomach, choking, or a feeling that he or she can't breathe.

Some fear is normal in most children, but an unexpected

onset of fear or patterns of strong fears and anxieties should be explored thoroughly.

Sexual symptoms. These can include things like abnormal anxiety about having genitals washed, excessive genital play, boldness in touching the genitals of other children, or becoming sexually seductive beyond the child's age level. A child may "know" too much about sexual behavior between adults and may describe involvement in sexual acts or the filming of sexual activity.

Vaginal or anal pain should prompt an immediate visit to a physician.

Emotional changes. Watch for emotional behavior that has not been normal for the child—anger, rage, a desire to hurt others, threatening to kill family members. The child may mutilate dolls, cutting off the heads, or want to use a knife destructively.

Be wary of sudden unexplainable mood changes such as temper tantrums. Note if a child becomes withdrawn or lethargic, showing no interest in anything. Some children may become overcompliant with parents or authority figures. Others may become hyperactive, depressed, or show an inability to learn or remember what has been said.

Physical symptoms. Watch for somatic complaints such as nausea or stomach pain, fear of swallowing saliva, fear of having to eat feces or drink urine. Physical weakness with no energy or total listlessness should be investigated.

The list of symptoms could be longer, but the principle is to pay attention to sudden changes in personality, likes and dislikes, fear and anxiety levels, or other departures from the normal patterns of the child.

RESPONDING TO A VICTIMIZED CHILD

Responding lovingly to a child who has been the victim of satanic ritual abuse is a real challenge. Behavior changes in the child—rebellion, abusive language, destructive actions—are difficult to live with. Parents must try to sort out what is motivating negative behaviors and respond appropriately.

Is the behavior a response to emotional and physical abuse? When hurt, a child may react in anger and that anger is often directed at parents who didn't cause the pain.

Is the behavior demonically empowered? For example, a child who never used profanity but begins swearing continuously may actually be in the control of a demon. Parents should not overreact to demonic activity, but take authority over it and cast it out in Jesus' name. Night terrors and frightening nightmares may also be the result of demonic activity.

It is not easy to separate the emotional aberration of a child, the programming infused by satanic abusers, and actual demonic activity. It will take time, patience, and careful listening to begin to unravel the sources of negative behavior. Parents can use a variety of strategies to help identify the source of problems and free their child.

Provide Love, Reassurance, and Control

When a child has been viciously victimized by satanists, the trust he had in his parents is severely damaged. Satanic programming has told the child, "Your parents don't love you. You deserve to be punished. You are bad. You are evil. Only Satan loves you."

Parents must avoid falling into a pattern of physical threats, spanking, or isolation to control unwanted behavior. There is a difference between punishment and discipline. Punishment inflicts retribution and causes hurt, but discipline provides safety and control. Its purpose is to re-train.

When dealing with children who are out of control, I often hold them in my arms so they feel the strength I have as security. I continually and gently tell them that no one is going to hurt them, and that I will not allow them to hurt anyone else. I tell them that God loves them and will heal them. Often programming will cause children to disbelieve this and to swear at God. I don't admonish them for this, but say, "God will never stop loving you, and He will heal you."

Swearing at God reveals the programming used by satanists through hypnosis, drugs, food and sleep deprivation, pain, and isolation. When this programming can be brought to conscious awareness, it will begin to lose its power.

A common disciplinary practice is to send a child to his room, saying, "You will have to stay there until you can behave." Unfortunately, a ritually abused child has terrifying memories of being put alone in a coffin, cage, or hole, so isolation in his bedroom will simply be too terrifying.

The ritually abused child needs discipline, not punishment. This child needs parents who consistently set limits and teach that behaviors have consequences. But the consequences imposed by parents should be moderate and logically linked to the behaviors needing change. For example, if a child refuses to pick up his toys, he should be told the consequence will be that he cannot play with them the next time. The next time he asks for the toys, remind him of his previous choice and help him understand its impact.

The key to discipline is consistency and reason. It is very important that the child develop the inner emotional security that consistent limits and reasonable discipline provide.

Use Spiritual Authority

As parents, God has appointed you the primary source of protection and spiritual authority over your home and family. You will need God's help in healing and setting your child free.

Begin by examining your own personal relationship with Jesus Christ as your Savior and Lord. Clean up the sin in your life. Read the Word of God and act on it. The books of Luke and Acts will help you understand your authority in Christ to heal and set free. A number of psalms will also encourage you. They speak of comfort and victory over sickness and evil: 6, 18, 23, 25, 27, 30, 31, 35, 37, 40, 46, 56, 57, 63, 66, 68, 91, 103, 104, 107, 118, 144, 145, 146, 147, and 148.

Listen to your abused child and don't feel the need to give answers right away. Let your child talk about her fears. Respect the fear that you as parents will be killed by the satanists if your child tells what happened. Remember, she may have witnessed human or animal sacrifice.

Respect the healing process and don't try to force your child to progress too fast. Your child will be checking to see if it is still safe to talk.

Believe your child if she talks of people wearing costumes, acting out fairy tales, or dressing in Halloween masks to create an unbelievable story of what would happen to her if she disclosed anything she witnessed.

Take authority over your home as a parent, binding and rebuking any demonic spirits and casting them out in the name of Jesus. Pray to God the Father to send warrior angels and ministering angels to give you protection and peace.

Pray for the power of the Holy Spirit to fill you and flow through you to your child. Lay hands on your child and pray for the Holy Spirit to heal the hurts. Bind and cast out every evil spirit in the name of Jesus, sending them to the bottomless pit. Break all curses of sickness, infirmity, and death put on your child and command all demons assigned to the curses to flee.

Remember the words of Zechariah 4:6: "Not by might, nor by power, but by my Spirit, says the Lord of Hosts—you will succeed because of my Spirit, though you are few and weak" (TLB).

Because satanic ritual abuse is becoming more public, you may be able to find a Christian counselor or minister to help you. By all means, search until you find the help you need. Get prayer support from friends or a prayer group, and attend a Bible-believing church where people will support you in your efforts to free your child.

HEALING FOR ADULT SURVIVORS

Healing for adult survivors of satanic ritual abuse is a very long process as one layer of pain after another is brought to the surface for healing. To complicate matters, demonic spirits are often hooked into the painful memories. The first challenge is to help survivors remember what really happened.

Recovering Memories

The process of recovering memories begins with a survivor being overwhelmed by emotions of depression, helplessness, and often intense physical pain. Through these sensations, a vague impression of a memory begins to emerge. Flashbacks or fragments of memories may follow. There is an ominous sense that something horrible happened to the person during childhood. There may be terrifying nightmares, and then the questioning, "Was that just a nightmare, or a memory from the past?"

More and more flashbacks and memories of burning candles, chanting people in black robes, upside-down crosses, an altar and blood and pain and screams of terror begin to come. A painful cry emerges, "Where were you, Mom and Dad, when I needed protection?" and then the horrifying realization that Mom and Dad themselves were the people in black robes. They were the ones hurting me, raping me. These repressed memories of the involvement of parents are often the hardest for a survivor to accept. Denial is strong, and they are confused with the other legitimate memories of their parents' involvement in a regular Christian church.

A child growing up with satanic parents is exposed to extreme abuse and incredible mind control. If by the grace of God the child survives to adulthood, it will often be because he has imposed a kind of amnesia on his memories. As this amnesia lifts, the pain of acknowledgment is indescribable.

Finding Freedom

In order to be free from satanism, the survivor must first accept Jesus Christ as personal Lord and Savior. Once I am certain of my clients' commitment, I lead them through a series of things to renounce.

- I renounce all pacts and covenants any of my ancestors made promising that all children born are dedicated to Satan and will serve him forever.
- I renounce my baptism in blood that I belong to Satan, and I renounce all words I have spoken saying that I give myself to Satan and make him my lord and god.
- I renounce all blood covenants and pacts I have signed giving my soul to Satan.
- I renounce all pacts to participate in black masses and human sacrifice.
- I renounce all satanic demons of power that have been given to me.
- I renounce being the bride of Satan, and I cast down

and break all oaths and agreements I made when I became a bride of Satan.

A confession of sin and granting absolution are important. Ask God for forgiveness for renouncing the Father,
Son, and Holy Spirit and claiming Satan as lord and god. A
confession of all participation in rituals such as the Black
Mass, human sacrifice, cannibalism, or abortion is essential. Many rituals are conducted by participating satanists
circling the victim in a satanic circle.

I take authority in the name of Jesus to break the power
of the satanic circle over the victim's life. I anoint the forehead with oil and break all curses and bondages, casting
out all demons assigned to them. If the survivor has any
marks or tattoos on her body, such as an inverted cross, I
pray to release her from their power.

A person who survives the training to become a satanist
is given special gifts by Satan. These can be things like the
gift of healing, extrasensory perception, clairvoyance, the
ability to control bleeding, or the power to stir up a whirl-
wind. All special gifts of Satan must be renounced. If unsure whether a gift is from Satan or God, I suggest that all
gifts be given back to God, and let Jesus return those He
wants to bestow.

One further complicating factor is present in many adult
survivors of satanic ritual abuse: the phenomenon of multiple personality disorder.

MULTIPLE PERSONALITY DISORDER

In working with SRA survivors I have discovered that
many also have multiple personality disorder (MPD). During my academic training I was taught that I would probably never encounter a patient with MPD in clinical
practice. The only books I had read on the subject were the
well-known *Sybil* and *The Three Faces of Eve*. Today, how-

ever, all across the country therapists working with the ritually abused are also learning how to treat multiple personality disorder.

SRA survivors experienced unbelievable physical and emotional abuse in early childhood. In order to survive the pain, an abused child often uses a coping mechanism called "dissociation"; she creates a new personality to deal with the pain. In this way, she can protect the core, or birth, personality with a self-induced amnesia and form a second, less vulnerable personality to experience the trauma for her.

Jennie Catherine Bloxson, a SRA survivor who developed MPD described her experience:

> When a very young child is subjected to pain and horror that is more than a brain and body can bear, the child dies. Or, if the child is young enough and creative enough, she can split her personality, much as a cell divides, and become another person. The new person endures and keeps the memory of the torturous event, leaving the child alive to continue.
>
> This ability surely comes from God as He alone can create new life. Why one child dies and another splits is known only to God.[1]

A clinical definition of multiple personality disorder can be found in the American Psychological Association's *Diagnostic and Statistical Manual* of mental disorders (DSM-III):

1. The existence within an individual of two or more distinct personalities, each of which is dominant at a particular time.
2. The personality that is dominant at any particular time determines the individual's behavior at that time.
3. Each individual personality is complex and integrated

with its own unique behavior patterns and social relationships.[2]

A person with MPD is not psychotic. When she reports
hearing voices within she is sometimes assumed to be hallucinating and is treated with psychotropic drugs. However, this definitely is not the appropriate treatment for
multiple personality disorder.

Others make the mistake of assuming that the alternate
personalities of an MPD are demons. They are not, and
they cannot be "cast out." On the other hand, I have
known some instances when demons were mistaken for alternate personalities. Most often with ritual abuse survivors, if there are multiple personalities, there will also be
demonic involvement. Both must be recognized and
treated. Obviously appropriate diagnosis is critical to healing and deliverance.

The therapy for multiple personality disorder generally
falls into three phases: testing and discovery, recovery of
painful memories, and reintegration of personality.

PHASE ONE: TESTING AND DISCOVERY

For the person with MPD, the beginning phase of therapy is a crucial time of testing the patient-therapist relationship to see if it is safe and the therapist can be trusted. It is
critical that a person with multiple personalities be believed, especially when reliving a bizarre or horrible memory. The therapist can't hide behind therapeutic cliches,
saying, "I believe you believe what you tell me is true."
That approach simply won't be accepted by an MPD. Most
often with multiple personalities, the core personality is
unaware that the others exist, at least at the outset. She will
have doubts that she is an MPD, or that a memory just re-
lived is really true, for she has survived by denying the
truth of these memories. In one sense, the client is correct;

the memory didn't happen to *her,* it happened to another personality.

A Maze of Personalities

Each person with multiple personalities has organized her personalities into a comprehensive structure. Some are relatively simple, and some are extremely complex. In the early stages of treatment the challenge for the therapist in the early stages of treatment is to discern the structural organization, which will facilitate access to all the personalities.

Donna, whom we met in Chapter 7, was a satanic ritual abuse survivor whose parents had both been satanists. Her childhood years were an endless nightmare of torture, sexual abuse, and the destruction and control of her mind, emotions, will, and spirit. Donna survived unbelievable cruelty and pain by splitting off and becoming multiple personalities. She actually developed three hundred personalities that were organized into ten families of thirty personalities each. Family number one was dominant, and those personalities were in charge most of the time. Donna also had two personalities that I call "inner self helpers." They were the most knowledgeable of the other personalities and were very helpful in directing therapy.

The core, or birth, personality was Sarah, who started splitting at about two years of age. To reach the personalities in the other families, I would first ask to speak with Sarah, and then ask for the personality I wanted. Sometimes, due to very painful memories and stress in her daily life, Sarah would split and create a new personality. When this new personality took over, the inner self helpers didn't know who was in charge and would report a loss of time in which they did not know what was happening. For example, a new personality, Tia, did not know who I was and was also unaware that she was part of a multiple personality system.

Tia once became confused when I asked for Sarah. Tia suggested I call Sarah on the phone if I wanted to talk to her, so I acted as if I were calling Sarah on the phone; when I asked to speak to her, she finally appeared. Through this vehicle, I could then make Tia a part of the system of personalities.

There is a difference between personalities that have significant memories over many years and personality fragments that were created for a limited time or because of a single traumatic event. For example, one personality may absorb the pain of a part of a traumatic event, then split so that a different fragment of personality feels the next episode of pain, and then split again to another fragment to take the next painful part, and so on.

During the beginning phase of therapy I try to discover the purpose each personality serves and what happened when it split from the birth person.

Usually during this time, I will also encounter demonic reactions and interference. I focus on breaking the bondage of Satan in the life of each personality, moving ultimately toward full release and integration.

PHASE TWO: RECOVERY OF PAINFUL MEMORIES

The middle phase of treatment is the longest, because it deals with the recovery of memories so vivid and painful they are almost as severe as experiencing the trauma for the first time. This process can only be endured by the client slowly, and it can go on for years. The survivor will be depressed and discouraged, because the memories seem never-ending. Each little respite is followed by another memory that cries for expression and healing.

As each memory is uncovered, prayer and the healing work of the Holy Spirit are essential. This is the primary difference between Christian and secular treatment approaches.

Satanic Programming

During this time some of the brainwashing of the satanists that systematically attempted to break the child's will
and control her will be uncovered.

I have come to believe that satanists purposely create
multiple personalities in children. Torture and training begin when a child is two years old so the child will be forced
to split and form new personalities. The personalities are
then trained in satanic rites and rituals. Future leaders are
selected because of their ability to split and endure pain
without complaint.

If a child is tortured and cries, she is severely punished.
More painful torture and abuse are administered until the
child learns to split and endure without any tears. Then the
child is rewarded.

The use of systematic torture produces a child who will
keep secrets and will have personalities trained in rituals
and rites that the birth personality will know nothing
about. Satanists do this not just because it works, but because demons inside them have a craving to see humans
tortured, raped, and sacrificed.

Constant Crisis

Working with survivors who have multiple personalities
is like living in a state of constant crisis. The power of the
memories with their intense pain is so overwhelming that
to the patient the experience feels nothing like healing. The
SRA survivor desperately wants to escape the pain by seeking relief through suicide. Because of the long process of
healing, the therapist can't afford to hospitalize an SRA survivor every time he or she is suicidal or in a state of crisis.
What is required is close monitoring and much support if a
crisis erupts and needs to be resolved.

There are periods when the survivor or one of her personalities becomes very self-abusive and feels the need to

punish herself for all the guilt and shame she feels. The personality may have been trained to burn herself with an iron, cigarettes, or boiling water, believing she is evil and needs to be punished. The self-abuse is perceived by the personality as the only relief for all the tension and anxiety she is experiencing.

Breaking Down Walls

As the healing continues, the walls separating various personalities become permeable, and what one personality is experiencing and feeling will be experienced by the others. This is especially true for the birth personality. This is a major sign of healing, but it is also a time of confusion because the protective walls no longer isolate the emotional trauma of each personality. If one is very depressed, the others will feel it also. When a rage that has been denied and split off into other personalities begins to surface, it creates a crisis, because the power of the rage is so awesome and overwhelming that the entire personality system feels out of control.

During the process of healing, a ritual abuse victim may have powerful and painful "body memories." Areas of the body that were previously injured may reexperience the pain just as if it were presently happening. Not only do the victims reexperience the pain, however, sometimes the marks of the injury reappear. On the face of a woman who had been struck so violently that her jaw was fractured, black and blue marks in the shape of a fist reappeared during her healing. Another woman's body memories caused her to have convulsive seizures, but her EEG test was normal and antiseizure medication was powerless to control the convulsions. She had suffered seizures as a child when she was tortured with electrical shocks and the injection of air into her spinal column.

During Donna's healing, her seven-year-old personality was reliving the memories of her torture during Holy Week when she was to live out the sufferings and crucifixion of Jesus. I was warned that having lived through the experience the first time wasn't a guarantee she would survive it a second time. Donna has survived her torture by splitting, but in reliving the experience as part of her healing, she would not split to another personality. The body memories of being scourged were so vivid, she had to wrap a towel around her back to absorb the blood. And when she recalled being nailed on a cross, both her wrists bled.

The pain victims experience in conjunction with the emotionally traumatic memories can be excruciating. During these times I believe that ritual abuse survivors could benefit from pain medication to help them survive the memories and prevent further splitting off of new personalities. It's difficult, though, to convince a physician to prescribe medication for a twenty-year-old injury.

PHASE THREE: REINTEGRATION

Reintegrating all the personalities into the birth personality is the final stage of healing. The sum total of all the memories, feelings, experiences, talents, skills, and learning that were previously located in the various personalities will be integrated back into one core personality.

The process of integration is a natural outcome of the healing of the memories in the personalities. There is a powerful desire in most MPDs to be healed and made whole. Integration is not difficult once the healing of memories has taken place and the personalities are eager for wholeness.

There are times, however, when an MPD is reluctant to give up a system that has functioned for most of her life. The distinct personalities are like children to her, and to have them integrated into the birth personality, losing their uniqueness, can be very threatening. Time must be taken so all are in agreement that complete healing is the goal.

It is often important to begin the integration of some personalities to help reduce the total number and to strengthen the birth personality by bringing coping skills from other personalities to the core.

During the final stage of healing and complete integration, the survivor will need supportive therapy. The integrated personality with new talents, skills, and memories must learn how to function in the world without resorting to splitting or dissociation to cope with life's traumas.

JESUS, THE ULTIMATE HEALER

Many survivors experience a painful blackness during the final process of healing the profound wounds of the past. It is a pain beyond any pain—a pain without words, without memories—that comes from the very depths of the soul. It can be so overwhelming that the victim has no strength to go on. Death becomes a welcome relief from the intense pain that vibrates through every cell in the body, every organ, every emotion. It is the dark night of the soul. No words can comfort, no person can help, and God—God is awesomely silent. The darkness is black on black. Tears come from unknown depths within. There is nothing to hold on to—and no hope—only despair, resignation, and death.

So you let go. You have no strength to go on living. You don't know if God will catch you in His mighty hand, yet you feel you must let go. You can't go on.

Then, somehow, someone is with you in your dark night of the soul, in your aloneness and unbearable pain. It is Jesus, who has experienced not only crucifixion, but God's silence. Christ's ultimate aloneness was so poignantly wrenched from His soul with the cry, "My God, My God, why have You forsaken Me?" (Mark 15:34). This stark aloneness was genuine; yet Jesus finally said, "Father, into Your hands I commit My spirit" (Luke 23:46).

Because Jesus experienced the incredible pain of the cross, because He "humbled Himself and became obedient to death—even death on a cross" (Phil. 2:8), He can be with you in your pain and your dark night of the soul. The Man of sorrows has walked through that darkness before you.

> Surely He has borne our griefs
> And carried our sorrows;
> Yet we esteemed Him stricken,
> Smitten by God, and afflicted.
> But He was wounded for our transgressions,
> He was bruised for our iniquities;
> The chastisement for our peace was upon Him,
> And by His stripes, we are healed.
>   (Isa. 53:4–5)

14

A CALL TO ARMS

I began this book by describing how God led me into ministry as a church pastor, then to become a licensed clinical psychologist, and finally to serve Him as an exorcist. As I look back, I see His hand working in my life, guiding and directing me, pushing me on, even when I was reluctant. And at times I was very reluctant.

I didn't want to be embarrassed or publicly humiliated or held up for ridicule. I didn't want my family to suffer. I didn't want to be called "a nut." I certainly didn't want to be at the center of controversy. I wanted simply to be an obedient servant and someday to approach the end of my earthly life knowing I had been faithful.

An obedient, faithful servant—that is what God asks each one of us to be. That is all He asks, and it is everything.

In dark moments when my human courage was weak, I would ask, "Why me, Lord? Why should I battle the forces of evil? I'm only one man. What good can I do when the cost of discipleship is so high?"

He always answered, "Why not you? I'll give you the courage you need and I'll show you what to do."

Through the years He has brought scores of hurting, suffering victims of Satan's evil to me and shown me how to engage and cast down the forces of darkness that would destroy those lives for all eternity. He made me a warrior and sent me into battle. Yet the victories aren't mine; they are His.

This book is another of God's victories. I don't know how He will use it or what good it will do, but I know He directed me to write it. He laid on my heart the need to reveal these experiences with Satan's evil warriors and to call the Church into the battle.

Still I asked, "Why me, Lord? Why should I write this book? What good can it do? I'm only one man."

As before, He answered, "Why not you? I'll give you the courage you need, and I'll show you what to do."

Then He reminded me of His words in Ezekiel:

Son of Man, speak to the children of your people, and say to them: "When I bring the sword upon a land, and the people of the land take a man from a territory and make him their watchman, when he sees the sword coming upon the land, if he blows the trumpet and warns the people, then whoever hears the sound of the trumpet and does not take warning, if the sword comes and takes him away, his blood shall be on his own head. . . .

"But if the watchman sees the sword coming and does not blow the trumpet, and the people are not warned, and the sword comes and takes any person from among them, he is taken away in his iniquity; but his blood I will require at the watchman's hand."

So you, son of man: I have made you a watchman for the house of Israel; therefore you shall hear a word from My mouth and warn them for Me. (33:2–7)

Next God reminded me of His words in Joel:

> Proclaim this among the nations:
> "Prepare for war!

> Wake up the mighty men,
> Let all men of war draw near,
> Let them come up . . .
> Let the weak say, 'I am strong' . . .
> Put in the sickle, for the harvest is ripe.
> Come, go down;
> For the winepress is full,
> The vats overflow—
> For their wickedness is great." (3:9–13)

When I read these words, I understood God's will clearly: I must write this book, revealing the full measure of evil I'd seen, warning of the danger of failing to take Satan's evil powers seriously, and calling the Church to engage itself in spiritual warfare against Satan and his evil warriors.

God also gave me another sign. He reminded me of a vision He had given me several years earlier when he told me that many in the Church are too content. They are comfortable with preaching against individual sin, but unwilling to face the reality of Satan's full power.

Contentment leads to complacency and complacency allows Satan's evil to succeed. He gleefully attacks and imprisons individuals, subjecting them to terrible abuses, horrifying pain, and eventual damnation, but that is not his real objective. Lucifer, the fallen angel, intends to destroy Christ's church and claim God's creation for himself.

In the vision God showed me a multitude of people with Jesus there among them. Christ's robe was dusty and dirty, but the smile on His face was radiant and loving. He was walking up a small desert hill, looking back and waving His arm, saying, "Come on." And the people were following Him. Some were running, some were limping on crutches, some were carrying those who couldn't walk. All of them were wounded and broken. It was evident each had come out of great pain, suffering, and bondage. They all had their eyes fixed on Jesus and their smiles of adoration and faith were overwhelming.

They are the victims, the ones who have personally experienced Satan's evil and through God's power have been healed and set free. They make a mighty army, for they know first-hand that Satan and his demons walk among us—ever ready to claim another soul, another family, another neighborhood, another city. They know the real meaning of Paul's words to the Ephesians:

Be strong in the Lord and in the power of His might. Put on the whole armor of God, that you may be able to stand against the wiles of the devil. For we do not wrestle against flesh and blood, but against principalities, against powers, against the rulers of the darkness of this age, against spiritual hosts of wickedness in the heavenly places. (6:10–12)

Paul was a watchman, who could see Satan's sword coming. He sounded the trumpet, calling the church at Ephesus to prepare for spiritual warfare. Paul "heard a word" from God's mouth and warned the people. But the warning wasn't just for the church at Ephesus or only for the people of Paul's earthly lifetime. Paul's warning is directed at all churches through time until the war with the forces of darkness is won.

He tells us to gird ourselves with truth and to shoe our feet with the gospel of peace, "above all, taking the shield of faith with which you will be able to quench all the fiery darts of the wicked one. And take the helmet of salvation, and the sword of the Spirit, which is the word of God; praying always with all prayer and supplication in the Spirit" (vv. 13–18).

God's Word, truth, faith, and prayer—these are our weapons. But to use them effectively, we must first know the truth.

FACT AND FICTION

Western scientific views, with the denial of the supernatural, are tragic fiction. These modern views of creation and the nature of evil are dangerous deceptions that aid Satan rather than stopping him.

Fact: Many modern thinkers believe the existence of Satan and his demons is a myth.

Fact: Satan is a totally evil, enormously powerful supernatural being who seeks to destroy God's creation and His people.

Fact: Many modern thinkers believe satanism is a social aberration that, although evil, is not a real threat. They believe it will die out naturally as society is enlightened by education.

Fact: Satanism is Satan's workplace. Through his worshipers he ensnares those who are vulnerable and unprotected.

Fact: Witchcraft, black magick, the Ouija board, Dungeons and Dragons and other fantasy games involving characters with evil and violent powers, common occult practices, such as astrology, channeling, tarot cards, healing crystals, seances, palm reading, astral travel, and EST, are subtle snares that can lead individuals directly to demonic activities.

Fact: Many modern thinkers, believing that psychotherapy and clinical psychology alone can heal people who are demonized, believe these people suffer only mental problems.

Fact: Psychotherapy and clinical psychology alone cannot free Satan's captives. Jesus Christ must intervene and victory is possible only through Him.

Fact: Although Satan's power is awesome, it is not equal to God's.

Fact: Satan and his horde cannot enter an individual's life and put the person in bondage without a legal right, such as the person's choice to continue in sin, traumatic emotional woundedness from his or her past, ancestral bondage due to Satanism, witchcraft, and curses, or the individual's involvement in the occult.

Fact: Exorcism is a real and viable method used by Christ to confront Satan's demons and release their victims from bondage.

Fact: Jesus Christ has given the Christian Church authority to rescue Satan's victims, bind the brokenhearted, and set the captives free.

Just as Paul said, we must stand firmly on God's Word, and armed with truth and faith we must engage Satan in spiritual warfare through intercessory prayer.

PRAYER WARRIORS

Monica's son, a gifted, talented young man, lived a life of unbridled sin. He was a drunk and lustful, interested only in self-satisfaction. Monica prayed constantly for her son, but he did not change. She went to her bishop and, crying bitter tears, poured out her heart. Through the bishop God spoke to Monica, telling her to go home and continue praying.

Monica's prayers were answered when her son found salvation. Eventually he became one of the fathers of the Christian Church. His name was Augustine.

Steve, a church pastor, worked for six years to build a

new congregation with little success. He and the church members prayed for the sick, but few got well. They prayed for the fellowship to grow and their labors for God to bear fruit, but only a few new members joined them. They began to pray without ceasing for the unsaved in the area around their church.

A demon of witchcraft appeared to Steve, claiming dominion over the geographical area and demanding that Steve and his church members stop bothering it. Through intercessory prayer Steve engaged the demon in spiritual warfare. He named the city streets of the neighborhood and in the name of Jesus commanded the demon to give up the territory and leave.

During the next three months the congregation doubled in size, and most of the converts needed to be delivered from witchcraft.

The prayers of righteous men and women are powerful and effective. They are our most potent weapons in fighting the forces of darkness. We must use these weapons and pray without ceasing, asking God to block Satan's warriors and send them back to the bottomless pit. We must pray for each other, especially those we know who are struggling. We must pray for our families, asking God to protect us from Satan's evil. We must pray for our neighborhoods, asking God to block and cast down those evil forces trying to establish strongholds. We must pray for our cities, our states, our country, our world, asking God to intervene against Satan's army of evil ones who create chaos, confusion, poverty, and greed.

And we must pray for our churches. Some of them are struggling under Satan's oppression as his demons try to block the spiritual lives of these bodies of Christ, creating unbelief, apathy, division, and unforgiveness.

We know God answers prayer. In just the past few years we have seen evidence of His answers as we witnessed the fall of the Berlin Wall and the demise of Communism. Just think of they many years we have prayed and the many prayers God's people have offered, asking Him to release the captives of Communism.

We will know the power of pulling down Satan's strongholds when we pray continuously, with purpose, and without ceasing until our prayers are answered.

NOTES

Foreword

1. Cathryn Creno, "Cult Horrors Are Real to Survivors," *The Arizona Republic,* July 1, 1990.

2. Martin Luther, 1483–1546, "A Mighty Fortress Is Our God," Tr. by Frederick H. Hedge.

Chapter 1

1. "Deliver Us From Evil," General Audience of Pope Paul VI, 15 November 1972, as reprinted in *L'Osservatore Romano,* 23 November 1972, *Deliverance Prayer,* Matthew and Dennis Linn, Eds., (New York: Paulist Press, 1981), 10.

Chapter 2

1. Nandor Fodor, *Freud, Jung and Occultism* (New Hyde Park: University Books, 1971), 16.

2. William J. Sneck, Ph.D., "Evil and the Psychological Dynamics of the Human Person," in *Deliverance Prayer,* Matthew and Dennis Linn, Eds. (New York: Paulist Press, 1981), 124.

3. Kenneth J. Metz, Ph.D., "A Trilateral View of Deliverance: Contribution of Psychology, Theology, and Sociology," in *Deliverance Prayer,* Matthew and Dennis Linn, Eds. (New York: Paulist Press, 1981), 214.

4. Rudolf Bultmann, *Kerygma And Myth* (New York: Harper, 1961), 4–5.

5. Richard Lessner, "Raising the Devil," *The Arizona Republic,* 21 May 1983. Used by permission.

6. Phillip Schaff, *History of the Christian Church, Vol. VII: Modern Christianity. The German Reformation* (Grand Rapids: William B. Eerdmans, 1950), 334.

7. Schaff, 335.

8. Ronald D. Laing, *The Divided Self* (London: Pelican Books, 1960).

9. Viktor Frankl, *The Doctor and the Soul* (New York: Alfred A. Knopf, 1955), 280.

Chapter 3

1. Douglas Hill and Pat Williams, *The Supernatural* (New York: Hawthorn Books, 1965), 51, 54–55.

2. George Kallas, *The Real Satan* (Minneapolis: Augsburg, 1975), 78.

3. George Eldon Ladd, *The Gospel of the Kingdom* (Grand Rapids: William B. Eerdmans, 1959), 55.

4. Karl A. T. Vogt, *Johannes Burgenhagen Pomeranas* (Elberfield: Fridrichs, 1867) in John Warwick Montgomery, *Principalities and Powers* (Minneapolis: Bethany House, 1973), 185.

Chapter 4

1. C. S. Lewis, *The Screwtape Letters* (New York: MacMillan Publishing Company, 1982), 56.

2. Mike Warnke, *The Satan Seller* (South Plainfield: Bridge Publishing, 1972), 184.

3. Ted Schwarz and Duane Empey, *Is Your Family Safe? Satanism* (Grand Rapids: Zondervan, 1988), 121–131. Used by permission.

4. Exerpted from "60 Minutes" as broadcast 15 September 1985. © 1985 CBS News.

5. CBS News.

6. CBS News.

7. "A Parent's Primer on Satanism," *Woman's Day,* 11 November 1988.

8. Kurt Koch, *Occult Bondage and Deliverance* (Grand Rapids: Kregel Publications, 1970), 15–16.

9. Koch, 16.

10. Warnke, 85.

11. Gerald Brittle, *The Demonologist* (New Jersey: Prentice Hall, 1980), 102.

12. Kurt Koch, *Between Christ and Satan* (Grand Rapids: Kregel, 1971), 104.

13. James A. Pike, *The Other Side* (New York: Doubleday, 1968), 383.

14. Shirley MacLaine, *Out on a Limb* (New York: Bantam Books, 1983).

15. Texe Marrs, *Dark Secrets of the New Age* (West Chester: Crossway Books, 1987), 98–99.

16. Johanna Michaelson, *The Beautiful Side of Evil* (Eugene: Harvest House, 1982), 154.

17. Lewis, 56.

Chapter 5

1. D. G. Fulford, "A Pox on You," *The Daily News of Los Angeles,* 11 October 1988 reprinted in *The Arizona Republic,* 31 October 1988. Used by permission.

2. Hill and Williams, 225–226.

3. William Schnoebelen, *Wicca: Satan's Little White Lie* (Chino: Chick Publications, 1990).

4. Schnoebelen, 22.

5. Schnoebelen, 22.

6. Schnoebelen, 42.

7. Schnoebelen, 46.

8. Schnoebelen, 13.

9. Warnke, 185.

10. Koch, *Occult Bondage and Deliverance,* 22.

11. Hill and Williams, 181–182.

12. Hill and Williams, 182.

13. Hill and Williams, 182.

14. Migene Gonzalez-Wippler, *Rituals and Spells of Santeria* (New York: Original Publications, 1984), 8.

15. Larry Kahaner, *Cults That Kill* (New York: Warner Books, 1988), 119.

16. Joseph M. Murphy, *Santeria: An African American Religion* (Boston: Beacon Press, 1988), 39.

17. Gonzalez-Wippler, 10.

18. Gonzalez-Wippler, 10.

Chapter 6

1. Dr. Joel Norris and Jerry Allen Potter, "The Devil Made Me Do It," *Penthouse,* December 1985.

2. Norris and Potter.

3. Norris and Potter.

4. Maury Terry, *The Ultimate Evil* (New York: Doubleday, 1987).

5. Terry.

6. Colin Wilson, *Mysterious Powers* (London: Aldus Books, 1975), 102.

7. Wilson, 106.

8. Bob Larson, *Satanism: The Seduction of America's Youth* (Nashville: Thomas Nelson, 1989), 152–153.

9. Marrs, 85.

10. Marrs, 86.

11. Salem Kirban, *Satan's Angels Exposed* (Huntington Valley: Salem Kirban, 1980), 86–87.

12. Kirban, 149.

13. Kirban, 152.

14. Katherine Ranslund, "Hunger for the Marvelous: The Vampire Craze in the Computer Age," *Psychology Today,* November 1989, 34.

15. John Frattarola, "America's Best Kept Secret," *Passport Magazine,* Special edition 1986, 12.

16. Frattarola, 11.

17. *Woman's Day.*

18. *Woman's Day.*

19. Anton La Vey, *The Satanic Bible* (New York: Avon Books, 1969), 33.

Chapter 7

1. Susan Schindehatte and others, "After the Verdict," *People Weekly,* 5 February 1990, 73.

2. Schindehette, 70.

3. Catherine Gould, "Symptoms Characterizing Satanic Ritual Abuse Not Usually Seen in Sexual Abuse Cases in Preschool Age Children," Unpublished paper, 12011 San Vincente Blvd., Suite 402, Brentwood, CA 90049. Used by permission.

4. Maribeth Kaye, M.C.S.U. and Lawrence Klein, Ph.D., "Clinical Indicators of Satanic Cult Victimization," Unpublished paper. Used by permission.

5. *Believe the Children Newsletter,* Volume 5, Issue 1, Winter 1990, 3.

6. Frattarola, 7.

Chapter 8

1. Republic Wire Services, 6 March 1990, as compiled from reports by The Associated Press and the *New York Daily News*.

2. Republic Wire Service.

3. Republic Wire Service.

4. Francis MacNutt, "The Imperative Need for the Church's Involvement in a Deliverance Ministry," in *Deliverance Prayer,* Matthew and Dennis Linn, Eds. (New York: Paulist Press, 1981), 146.

5. Peter C. Wagner, *Your Spiritual Gifts* (Ventura: Regal Books, 1979).

Chapter 9

1. John White, "Problems and Procedures in Exorcism," *Demon Possession,* John Warwick Montgomery, Ed. (Minneapolis: Bethany House, 1976), 281–282.

2. Laing.

3. J. L. Nevius, *Demon Possession* (Grand Rapids: Kregel, 1968).

4. C. S. Lewis, "Christianity and Culture."

Chapter 13

1. Excerpted from a personal letter. Used by permission.

2. *The Diagnostic and Statistical Manual of Mental Disorders,* 3rd Edition (DSM-III), American Psychological Association, 1980.

BIBLIOGRAPHY

Brittle, Gerald. *The Demonologist*. New Jersey: Prentice Hall, 1980.

Bultman, Rudolf. *Kerygma And Myth*. New York: Harper, 1961.

Cruz, Nicky. *Devil On The Run*. Melbourne: Dove Christian Books, 1989.

Frankl, Viktor E., M.D. *The Doctor and the Soul*. New York: Knopf, 1955.

Freud, Sigmund. "A Neurosis of Demonical Possession in the Seventeenth Century." *Collected Papers*. Joanne Riviere, trans. London: Hogarth Press, 1949.

Gonzalez-Wippler, Migene. *Rituals and Spells of Santeria*. New York: Original Publications, 1984.

Hill, Douglas, and Pat Williams. *The Supernatural*. New York: Hawthorn, 1965.

Kahaner, Larry. *Cults That Kill*. New York: Warner Books, 1988.

Kallas, James. *The Real Satan*. Minneapolis: Augsburg, 1975.

Kirban, Salem. *Satan's Angels Exposed*. Huntington Valley: Salem Kirban, 1980.

Koch, Kurt. *Between Christ and Satan*. Grand Rapids: Kregel, 1962.

———. *Occult Bondage and Deliverance*. Grand Rapids: Kregel, 1970.

Ladd, George Eldon. *The Gospel of the Kingdom*. Grand Rapids: Eerdmans, 1959.

Laing, R. D. *The Divided Self*. London: Pelican, 1960.

Larson, Bob. *Satanism: The Seduction of America's Youth*. Nashville: Thomas Nelson, 1989.

Lewis, C. S. *The Screwtape Letters*. New York: MacMillan, 1982.

Marrs, Texe. *Dark Secrets of the New Age*. West Chester: Crossway, 1987.

Martin, Malachi. *Hostage to the Devil*. New York: Reader's Digest Press, 1976.

Montgomery, John Warwick, ed. *Demon Possession*. Minneapolis: Bethany House, 1976.

Murphy, Joseph M. *Santeria: An African American Religion*. Boston: Beacon, 1988.

Nevius, J. L. *Demon Possession*. Grand Rapids: Kregel, 1968.

Peck, M. Scott, M.D. *The People of the Lie*. New York: Simon and Schuster, 1983.

Pike, Bishop James A. *The Other Side*. New York: Doubleday, 1968.

Schaff, Phillip. *History of the Christian Church, Volume VII. Modern Christianity. The German Reformation*. Grand Rapids: Eerdmans, 1950.

Schwarz, Ted, and Duane Empey. *Is Your Family Safe? Satanism*. Grand Rapids: Zondervan, 1988.

Terry, Maury. *The Ultimate Evil*. New York: Doubleday, 1987.

Wagner, C. Peter. *Your Spiritual Gifts*. Ventura: Regal, 1979.

Warnke, Mike. *The Satan Seller*. South Plainfield: Bridge Publishing, 1972.

Wilson, Colin. *Mysterious Powers*. London: Aldus Books, Danbury Press, a division of Gudier Enterprises, 1975.

✳

ABOUT THE AUTHOR

Ken Olson, nationally known speaker and author of five books, is a clinical psychologist and Lutheran minister. He serves The Center for Living in Phoenix, Arizona. He holds the B.S. in psychology and the Ed.D. in counseling psychology from Arizona State University and the Master of Divinity from Northwestern Lutheran Theological Seminary, and is the recipient of "Continuance Professus Articulatus Excellence," the highest award given by The National Speakers Association. His previous books include *The Art of Hanging Loose in an Uptight World, I Hurt Too Much for a Band Aid,* and *The Art of Staying Well in an Uptight World.*

He lives in Paradise Valley, Arizona, with his wife, Jean. They are the parents of three grown children, Michael, Daniel, and Janet.